P9-BXZ-525

WHY CHURCHES DIE

WHY CHURCHES DIE
Diagnosing Lethal Poisons in the Body of Christ

MAC BRUNSON & ERGUN CANER

BROADMAN
&HOLMAN
PUBLISHERS

NASHVILLE, TENNESSEE

Copyright © 2005
by Mac Brunson and Ergun Caner

All rights reserved
Printed in the United States of America

Ten-Digit ISBN: 0–8054–3181–0
Thirteen-Digit ISBN: 978–0–8054–3181–0

Published by Broadman & Holman Publishers
Nashville, Tennessee

Dewey Decimal Classification: 262
Subject Heading: CHURCH CONFLICT \
SPIRITUAL LIFE

Scripture quotations have been taken from the *Holman Christian Standard Bible®* Copyright © 1999, 2000, 2002, 2004 by Holman Bible Publishers. Used by permission. Italic in Scripture text has been added by the authors for emphasis.

10 9 8 7 6 5 4 3 2 1   10 09 08 07 06 05

Dedication

The authors would like to dedicate this book to all
the churches they have served through the years:

Mac served:

First Baptist Church of Damascus, Greenwood, South Carolina
South Norfolk Baptist Church, Chesapeake, Virginia
Green Street Baptist Church, High Point, North Carolina
First Baptist Church of Dallas, Dallas, Texas

Ergun served:

Manchester Baptist Church, Manchester, Kentucky
Ridgecrest Baptist Church, Vincennes, Indiana
Wood Baptist Church, Wood, North Carolina
Central Baptist Church, Aurora, Colorado
Thomas Road Baptist Church, Lynchburg, Virginia

Contents

Introduction

"Church Would Be Easy Without People"

Church would be a whole lot easier if it were not for the members. . . ."

It was an honest admission by a leading evangelical pastor, but quite frankly, it took us by surprise. The man had served some of the largest churches in our denomination, but in a weary moment, he admitted that in his heart of hearts, he hated pastoring.

Perhaps this statement is a bit strong. Perhaps it is better said that he loved the calling, but the tangential bureaucracy of modern church life drove him crazy.

The spats over bulletins.

The arguments over the color of choir robes.

The quarrels concerning parking lots.

The disputes over committees, deacons, and sermon length.

You get the point. It is a sad secret that many pastors secretly resign every Monday. They lie in bed, debating internally whether to get up or hide under the mattress.

Interestingly, many church members go through the same internal war. They faithfully attend church but quietly rue getting up on Sunday. They drag themselves to the building and attempt to invoke a smile that serves as a facade. The silliness and sinfulness that consumes many churches drive Christians to survive church.

These same machinations also cause many Christians to avoid church altogether. That is the purpose of this work. To identify the diseases that besiege local churches, excise the poisons, and bring church back to the biblical model . . . joyous and encouraging.

The Biblical Standard of "One Another"

Does the previous sentence seem too Pollyannaish to you? Is it unrealistic to desire to want church to be a place of spiritual edification? Not according to the biblical record. Throughout the New Testament, the biblical authors call local churches to specific action. One of the most enlightening studies is to examine the biblical teachings concerning our responsibilities to "one another." Notice we are called to:

1. Be in agreement with one another.

Romans 12:10: Show family affection to one another with brotherly love. Outdo one another in showing honor . . . 16: Be in agreement with one another. Do not be proud; instead, associate with the humble. Do not be wise in your own estimation.

2. Pursue that which builds up one another.

Romans 14:13: Therefore, let us no longer criticize one another, but instead decide not to put a stumbling block or pitfall in your brother's way . . . 19: So then, we must pursue what promotes peace and what builds up one another.

3. Accept one another.

Romans 15:5: Now may the God of endurance and encouragement grant you agreement with one another, according to Christ Jesus . . . 7: Therefore accept one another, just as the Messiah also accepted you, to the glory of God . . . 14: Now, my brothers, I myself am convinced about you that you also are full of goodness, filled with all knowledge, and able to instruct one another.

4. Show courtesy to one another.

1 Corinthians 11:33: Therefore, my brothers, when you come together to eat, wait for one another.

5. Carry one another's burdens.

Galatians 6:2: Carry one another's burdens; in this way you will fulfill the law of Christ.

6. Tolerate one another.

Ephesians 4:2: with all humility and gentleness, with patience, accepting one another in love . . .

7. Forgive one another.

Ephesians 4:32: And be kind and compassionate to one another, forgiving one another, just as God also forgave you.

Colossians 3:13: accepting one another and forgiving one another if anyone has a complaint against another. Just as the Lord has forgiven you, so also you must [forgive].

8. Submit to one another.

Ephesians 5:21: submitting to one another in the fear of Christ.

1 Peter 5:5: Likewise, you younger men, be subject to the elders. And all of you clothe yourselves with humility toward one another, because God resists the proud, but gives grace to the humble.

9. Admonish one another in wisdom.

Colossians 3:16: Let the message about the Messiah dwell richly among you, teaching and admonishing one another in all wisdom, and singing psalms, hymns, and spiritual songs, with gratitude in your hearts to God.

10. Comfort one another.

1 Thessalonians 4:9: About brotherly love: you don't need me to write you because you yourselves are taught by God to love one another . . . 18: Therefore encourage one another with these words.

1 Thessalonians 5:11: Therefore encourage one another and build each other up as you are already doing . . . 15: See to it that

no one repays evil for evil to anyone, but always pursue what is good for one another and for all.

11. Promote love and good works in one another.

Hebrews 10:24: And let us be concerned about one another in order to promote love and good works. . . .

12. Love one another.

1 Peter 1:22: By obedience to the truth, having purified your-selves for sincere love of the brothers, love one another earnestly from a pure heart. . . .

1 Peter 4:8–9: Above all, keep your love for one another at full strength, since love covers a multitude of sins. Be hospitable to one another without complaining.

1 John 3:11: For this is the message you have heard from the beginning: we should love one another . . . 23: Now this is His command: that we believe in the name of His Son Jesus Christ, and love one another as He commanded us.

1 John 4:7: Dear friends, let us love one another, because love is from God, and everyone who loves has been born of God and knows God . . . 11: Dear friends, if God loved us in this way, we also must love one another. 12: No one has ever seen God. If we love one another, God remains in us and His love is perfected in us.

It Is Harder Than It Sounds, Isn't It?

Looking over that list, one could easily become depressed. So many people attend church to be seen, to make connections, or to attack one another. Often it seems that the majority of people who profess to be Christians do not act as Christians. The situa-tion appears to be dire at best, hopeless at worst.

However, can it be that we are focusing on the worst among us? Is it not part of human nature to obsess over the negative aspects of church? Let us share a poorly kept secret among pas-tors. In most churches, we stand at the back door and shake hands, using a secret handshake. We take your right hand in ours, place our left hand on your elbow, and we then proceed to pull you out the door! We do this for any number of reasons, including the fact that a large number of people are standing behind you, and they are looking at their watches while you spend an hour telling us about your sick goldfish.

We are also aware that it is difficult to stand in the line. The church member is trying to think of something to say that does not sound trite and clichéd. Usually, the member says something gracious, such as "wonderful sermon" or "lovely day."

However . . .

Sometimes, one person decides to use that opportunity to drive a verbal knife into our heart. A quick word of criticism, usually said with a smile, digs deep. It could be that one hundred people were blessed by the sermon, but one person disliked it.

On whom do we focus?

The critic.

We are not alone in this dilemma. The half-brother of Jesus apparently had heard enough criticism, and under the inspiration of the Holy Spirit, he calls the church twice to cease criticism.

James 4:11: Don't criticize one another, brothers. He who criticizes a brother or judges his brother criticizes the law and judges the law. But if you judge the law, you are not a doer of the law but a judge.

James 5:9: Brothers, do not complain about one another, so that you will not be judged. Look, the judge stands at the door!

His point is clear—God will judge us by the measure we judge (and criticize) one another.

With this list of the "Holy Dozen," we endeavor to diagnose the most debilitating diseases in the body of Christ. Consider this an autopsy of churches that have died and a biopsy of churches that are seriously ill. However, we sincerely hope you consider, examine, and analyze these symptoms. We wish they were not epidemic. We pray they do not become lethal.

Chapter 1

Toxins and Terminal Diseases in the Body of Christ

Extending the Right Fist of Fellowship
1 Corinthians 3:1–4

Have you ever stood in a church parking lot and listened to a story that ended with one of these sentences?

"That church split over the color of the carpet!"

"She walked right up to the pulpit and slapped the pastor!"

"The deacons' meeting ended in an actual fist fight!"

Disturbing, isn't it? Local churches all over the world split so often that it is almost an assumed end. Pastors are fired, members storm off, staff members take a group from one church to start another just down the road. Business meetings become Christian versions of *Thunderdome.* Yelling, fighting, screaming. Taking sides against fellow believers. Doubting one another's salvation. Power plays, deception, and alliances that would rival any *Survivor* episode.

Have you ever stopped and asked yourself, "How in the world did we get here? Is this what church is supposed to be like?"

Have you ever wondered why members of the church of the living God sometimes act like nonbelievers?

Have you ever thought that church might be fun and fulfilling, were it not for the people inside the building?

Have you ever been so outraged by actions in the church that you swore off church completely?

Have you ever felt that going to church was a waste of your time?

Have you ever wondered why God would even save some of these folk, much less use them in leadership in a local church?

Well, so have we.

You read correctly. Two men, with a combined fifty years of pastoral experience, have been frustrated often by the churches we were called to serve. In truth, so are most pastors. When we gather in conventions and meetings, ministers often speak in hushed tones and whispers, relaying stories of horrific business meetings, contentious committees, and brutal fellowships. And dear reader, if we were to be painfully honest, so can we all.

Virtually every Christian, active in a local assembly, can share stories that defy the imagination. Church is not supposed to be this way.

Church: The Way Things Ought to Be

The biblical description of the church does not include any of the wars, fights, and furies. In the seventy-seven references to "church" in the Bible, we find an empowered people of God, left as ambassadors to the world and family to one another. In the days following Pentecost, the unity that exemplified the newly formed body of believers would cause many present-day churches shame in comparison. Notice Luke's description in Acts 2:42–47:

And they devoted themselves to the apostles' teaching,
to fellowship, to the breaking of bread, and to prayers.
Then fear came over everyone, and many wonders and
signs were being performed through the apostles. Now
all the believers were together and had everything in
common. So they sold their possessions and property
and distributed the proceeds to all, as anyone had a
need. And every day they devoted themselves [to meet-
ing] together in the temple complex, and broke bread
from house to house. They ate their food with gladness
and simplicity of heart, praising God and having favor
with all the people. And every day the Lord added
those who were being saved to them.

Examine the descriptive titles for the church. God's owner-
ship of the church certainly bespeaks our stewardship. The
church is called:

- holy (1 Cor. 1:2),
- the body of Christ (Rom. 12:5; 1 Cor. 12:12, 27; Eph. 3:6;
  4:12; 5:23; Col. 3:15),
- God's household (1 Tim. 3:15),
- the pillar and foundation of the truth (1 Tim. 3:15),
- church of the living God (1 Tim. 3:15), and
- church of the firstborn (Heb. 12:23).

Furthermore, Christ's relationship to his church is remark-
able. He did not leave us without instruction or provision. From
Peter's confession at Cesarea Philippi until now, Christ's position
is seminal. To the church, Christ is called the head of the church
(Eph. 1:22–23; 5:23) and the head of the body (Col. 1:18). He
builds the church upon the rock of our confession (Matt.
16:15–18), and cares for the church (Eph. 5:29). Paul is
emphatic — Christ's love for his body is so profound that he gave
himself for it (Eph. 5:25).

In the book of Acts, and in fact the entire embryonic days of
the church, local fellowships were warm and inviting families,
often given to extraordinary acts of generosity and love.

- The churches at Macedonia and Achaia helped Paul when he was in need (Rom. 15:26; 2 Cor. 11:9).
- The church at Thessolonica served as a "model to all believers" and had been taught by God to love one another (1 Thess. 1:7; 4:10).
- The church at Philippi shared sacrificially with Paul when he lacked financial ability (Phil. 4:14–16).
- The church at Berea was known throughout the region for studying the Scriptures intently every day (Acts 17:10–12).
- The Lord did not have a word of rebuke against the church at Smyrna in John's seven admonitions. Of the seven churches listed in Revelation 2–3, Smyrna alone was described in a wholly positive light, and is even called "rich" (Rev. 2:8–11).

Though none of these churches were perfect, they were identified as local fellowships that did share a common bond and love. Do all churches measure up to that standard?

Tragically, no.

The Games Christians Play: The Church Search

Follow the journey of a young Christian couple, moving to a new town.

The husband and wife, having started a new job, have moved to a new town where they do not know anyone. Having been active in their church back home, they hope to find a church in their new town that has the same spirit and level of commitment. Without any leads, however, they must embark on one of the more prevalent games in our culture: the church search.

Over the course of months, they set out to visit a number of churches, hoping to find one to which they feel called and in which they will serve. The rules of this unspoken game are simple—make no promises, keep an open mind, observe everything, and "we will talk about it when we get back in the car." Do you recognize this game? You have probably played it, and did not even know it.

The first Sunday they walk into a magnificent structure. The church rises from the street with gothic wings and steeples. It is beautiful and breathtaking. The husband immediately notices that the grounds are immaculately manicured and well kept. Surely this is a good sign.

As they enter the church, the sounds of the organ rise to a crescendo. The wife loves this type of worship, so she smiles to herself. The husband is greeted in the foyer by an elderly gentleman who hands them a bulletin, printed with a beautiful sketch of the church on the front. The wife takes the two children by the hand and walks toward a greeter, hoping to check the children into the nursery. *"Nursery?"* the greeter wonders out loud. "We don't have a nursery," he says matter-of-factly. "A few years ago we had a day care center, but everything went wrong, and the deacons shut it down. We don't even use it anymore. It was too much trouble and too much expense."

Strike one.

The second church they visited was as friendly a place as the couple had ever seen. The nursery was alive with children and well lighted, with colorful paintings of Noah's ark and animals on the walls. The Sunday school class for the adults had doughnuts and coffee in the central room, and then the individual classes broke up into sections. The various class members joked and laughed easily and bespoke a warm friendship among the members. The teacher was personable and kind and had obviously studied the lesson. By the time the young couple walked upstairs to the auditorium for the worship service, they were both smiling and nodding in agreement. Perhaps they had found their church.

As the worship began, the music was profoundly moving. The instruments all worked together to provide a beautiful melody, and the words appeared on the screen above the platform. The wife was almost moved to tears even before the singing had begun. There was only one problem. The young couple had apparently been seated in the "loud and stubborn complainers' section."

As the praise team led the congregation in worship, the only thing louder than the singers was the chorus of complainers that surrounded the young couple.

"I can't stand this new stuff—it's just noise!" said one woman.

"He keeps calling it blended, but how do you blend good music with trash?" asked another.

"When was the last time we even used the hymnal?" queried a man in their pew.

For the young couple, it was clear. A split fellowship. Complainers.

Strike two.

The young couple decided to visit a smaller church the next week. *Surely in a smaller church there will not be all this fighting and contention,* they thought. As they parked on the gravel next to the country church, the husband smiled and spoke to his wife: "This reminds me of the church I grew up in." It was bringing back fond memories.

The nursery was smaller, for sure, but the woman who greeted the couple was cheerful and welcoming. The children seemed happy to play with her, and the couple walked down the hallway to the fellowship hall for their class. The teacher was plain-spoken, and wisdom seemed to emanate from him. The lesson was wonderful and meaningful to the couple, and they were welcomed by a half dozen people with a hearty handshake. As they climbed the stairs to the sanctuary, the husband and wife were greeted at the top by a gentleman with a bulletin. Inside the bulletin was a litany of prayer requests, announcements, and the offering, listed on the bottom right hand side.

The songs and singing reminded them both of services gone by, and they thoroughly enjoyed the service. The preaching was fervent, and the invitation saw a couple of people joined at the altar in prayer. *Was this too good to be true?* the couple thought as the service concluded.

Then a deacon rose to the pulpit and announced the monthly business meeting was in order. As the financial spreadsheets were passed out, the deacon/moderator quickly covered old minutes and old business in short fashion. Everything seemed to be perfunctory, until new business was introduced. Then an argument broke out over a line item for the mowing of the churchyard. One man wanted his son to mow the lawn and asked for the present worker to be fired. The discussion became heated quickly, and any warmth in the fellowship quickly dissipated.

Strike three.

Unfortunately, modern Christianity is marked by divided fellowships and uneasy truces. Many churches carry on as if the body of Christ was supposed to argue, fuss, and fight. Since churches have been arguing and splitting since time immemorial, why should we be any different?

Why indeed?

Spiritual Forensics: Symptoms and Diseases

If so many local churches die, and even more are paralyzed or terminally ill, can nothing be done? Perhaps it is possible to perform a spiritual autopsy to examine the root causes for their untimely deaths.

Why have so many churches experienced so many problems?

Why do Christians, many of whom have been raised and trained in godly churches and under biblical preaching, end up acting like pagans—*in the church*?

How can churches that normally act in a godly manner all of a sudden break out into a festering fellowship of fighting, bickering, and splits?

Why is it almost normative to see backbiting and gossip in every church?

Because the majority of churches and the majority of Christians are infected with a disease, and they have gone untreated for too long. These diseases and pathologies are not physical. In fact, in many ways they are far more noxious than physical diseases. They are spiritual diseases—spiritual diseases in the body of Christ.

A spiritual disease or pathology is often undetectable, except for the telling symptoms. Christians often can be infected with this disease and show very few symptoms. These people are *carriers*. Like Typhoid Mary, the carrier of a spiritual disease spreads his contagion to virtually everyone whom they touch. In the church this person is the instigator. In every church they serve, fights break out, fellowships are destroyed, and the carrier walks away like an innocent victim, acting as if he had nothing to do with the battle. Carriers are in every church.

As in physical diseases, symptoms are the telltale signs that indicate a spiritual disease is present. The difficult task is to examine the symptoms with clarity. The most difficult task is to perform self-examination. Though this book will often examine humorous events, do not allow the humor to dissuade you. The events herein actually happened. Though we have changed the names and locations to protect the infected, they actually took place, and often with tragic results. Perhaps we have become inoculated against such things because we have seen them so frequently. Live with lepers for too long, and you stop noticing the sores. We pray that is not the case.

The good news to the Christian is this: Every one of these maladies is treatable. You do not have to succumb to the ravages and damages of the spiritual illness. You must, however, actually act to stop the onslaught of the disease. These infections and poisons exist in churches across our land. It is time to treat the illness and stop the infections.

Ephesus: A Schizophrenic and Lethal Fellowship

Virtually every church suffers from spiritual setbacks on occasion, but most Christians believe their situation is unique. They cannot fathom how any church could come to such a sad state of affairs. They feel they are alone in their problems. "Other churches do *not* fight like this," they lament. They feel like they have somehow stumbled into the *only* churches in Christendom filled with power brokers, politicians, and weak leaders.

Wrong.

Even in the Bible, there were churches that were not exemplary in character and deed. They fought, bickered, slandered one another, jockeyed for position, and built alliances against one another. Let us examine a couple of instances where the churches were not the perfect biblical example. Case in point: *Ephesus*.

Paul first visited this commercial and political center of western Asia at the end of his second missionary journey. Located on the western coast of what is now Turkey, Ephesus was a great port city, and thus it was a strategic location for a church. The city was highly religious and given to idolatry, as the temple of Diana (the Greeks called her Artemis) was located there. If Paul could plant a church there on the major coast of the Mediterranean Sea, the church would become a gateway city from which to launch other churches.

In Acts 18:19–28, Paul arrived at Ephesus, and he preached at the synagogue in the city. Having to return to Antioch, Paul promised to return to the city soon. To help begin the work, he left his traveling companions, Priscilla and Aquila, in Ephesus. They soon won a Jewish philosopher and scholar named Apollos to Christ. Before the church was even a few months old, Apollos became their first missionary, going to Achaia to present Christ in the synagogues (Acts 18:24–28). So far so good. The church in Ephesus was just a small body of believers, but already they had strong leaders and a definite vision for spreading the gospel.

As Paul began his third and final missionary journey, he came back to Ephesus, where he would spent the next two and one-half years. Paul poured his energies into the church there, and the efforts were fruitful. Some disciples of John the Baptist who were looking for the Messiah were saved (Acts 19:1–7). For three months, Paul debated in the Ephesian synagogue and almost caused a riot. Some of the leaders in the synagogue were so offended by his teachings that he had to move to the lecture hall of Tyrannus, where he began a two-year ministry of teaching and debate (Acts 19:8–10).

If ever there was a *seeker-motivated* church, with unique outreach ministries and an effective cultural strategy, it was Ephesus in its early years. Luke speaks of an amazing work during those days: "This went on for two years, so that all the inhabitants of the province of Asia, both Jews and Greeks, heard the word of the Lord" (Acts 19:10).

The first major crisis that faced the Ephesian church was external. The seven sons of a Jewish chief priest named Sceva were attempting to cast out demons, as they had seen Paul do so often. As Paul had been seen doing miraculous works, the power of God was being tested. Could anyone—pagan or Christian—cast out demons simply by reciting the mantra they had heard? The showdown between the demonic realm and Sceva's pagan sons was horrific:

> Then some of the itinerant Jewish exorcists attempted to pronounce the name of the Lord Jesus over those who had evil spirits, saying, "I command you by the Jesus whom Paul preaches!" Seven sons of Sceva, a Jewish chief priest, were doing this. The evil spirit answered them, "Jesus I know, and Paul I recognize— but who are you?" Then the man who had the evil spirit leaped on them, overpowered them all, and prevailed against them, so that they ran out of that house naked and wounded. (Acts 19:13–16)

The sight of seven naked, bleeding false prophets stumbling into the street, beaten by a demon that was mocking them, caused a revival to break out. Luke continues the amazing narrative:

> This became known to everyone who lived in Ephesus, both Jews and Greeks. Then fear fell on all of them, and the name of the Lord Jesus was magnified. And many who had become believers came confessing and disclosing their practices, while many of those who had practiced magic collected their books and burned them

in front of everyone. So they calculated their value, and found it to be 50,000 pieces of silver. In this way the Lord's message flourished and prevailed.
(Acts 19:17–20)

The consequence of such a wholesale abdication of idolatry profoundly affected commerce in Ephesus. In fact, a riot broke out. A silversmith named Demetrius gathered all the men in the craftsmen's union and brought charges against Paul. Demetrius said that Paul and the followers of Christ were blaspheming the goddess of the temple in Ephesus, and they were ruining the business of idolmakers. As the chanting crowds gathered in the Ephesian theater, Christian leaders of the Ephesian church such as Alexander, Gaius, and Aristarchus tried to present their case, but the entire city was in an uproar. The situation was so dangerous that even Paul's friends would not allow him to enter the theater because they feared for his safety. Were it not for the reasonable words of the city clerk, the entire Christian community in Ephesus might have perished (Acts 19:23–41).

One would think that any fellowship that was blessed to have Paul's undivided attention for thirty months, that had seen city-wide revival following a pagan challenge, that developed a region-wide reputation as a threat to the very economics of the city, and that had such luminary leaders as Priscilla and Aquila, would be a strong and steady church, demonstrating a genuine affection for one another, and demonstrating the power of God. But let's pause for a reality check.

The first hint that Ephesus may not have been a "perfect church" is found in Paul's first letter to the Corinthians. In the final chapter of the letter, Paul speaks of his future travel plans, including Corinth and Macedonia. But he also notes, "I will stay in Ephesus until Pentecost, because a wide door for effective ministry has opened for me—yet many oppose me" (1 Cor. 16:8–9). Whether that opposition was internal or external is not clear, but we soon realize that all is not as peaceful as Paul had hoped.

Paul's letter to the Ephesian church, written between AD 60 and 63, suggests that the unity for which he had labored so long was being threatened by divisive leaders who were teaching doctrines that were contrary to the Lord:

And He personally gave some to be apostles, some prophets, some evangelists, some pastors and teachers, for the training of the saints in the work of ministry, to build up the body of Christ, until we all reach unity in the faith and in the knowledge of God's Son, [growing] into a mature man with a stature measured by Christ's fullness. Then we will no longer *be little children,* tossed by the waves and blown around by every wind of teaching, by human cunning with cleverness in the techniques of deceit. (Eph. 4:11–14)

Was Paul actually calling this fellowship that was so dear to his heart "little children"? Were they acting contentiously and not treating one another with the love due to fellow believers in a local church? Look again at Paul's pointed admonition that follows:

No rotten talk should come from your mouth, but only what is good for the building up of someone in need, in order to give grace to those who hear. And don't grieve God's Holy Spirit, who sealed you for the day of redemption. All bitterness, anger and wrath, insult and slander must be removed from you, along with all wickedness. And be kind and compassionate to one another, forgiving one another, just as God also forgave you in Christ. (Eph. 4:29–32)

The church was apparently experiencing some malicious gossip that was coming from fellow believers in the church! Paul states emphatically that such acts as bitterness, rage, fighting, and gossip are violations of the love of Christ. Has your church ever experienced malicious gossip and rumor mongering? You are not alone.

Evidently, gossip was not the only problem besetting the church at Ephesus. Paul continues: "But sexual immorality and any impurity or greed should not even be heard of among you, as

is proper for saints. And coarse and foolish talking or crude jok-
ing are not suitable, but rather giving thanks. For know and recognize this: no sexually immoral or impure or greedy person,
who is an idolater, has an inheritance in the kingdom of the
Messiah and of God" (Eph. 5:3–5).

Was the Ephesian fellowship dealing with such issues as sexual immorality and greed? Paul seems to think so. As a matter of
fact, Paul commits a significant portion of his letter to all familial
relationships, such as those between husband and wife and children and parents (Eph. 5:21–6:4). Under the inspiration of the
Holy Spirit, Paul was authoring a literary rebuke of unparalleled
dimensions.

If Paul's first address to the Ephesian church seems to suggest deterioration in the fellowship, his letters to their pastor
removes all doubt. Though the exact date of 1 Timothy is
uncertain, we do know some time had passed since the found-
ing of the church. Alexander, who attempted to defend Paul in
the Ephesian theater in Acts 19, had succumbed to teaching
heresy. Paul states that along with Hymenaeus, Alexander had
"suffered the shipwreck of his faith," and Paul had "delivered
him to Satan so he might be taught not to blaspheme" (1 Tim.
1:19–20).

How damaging were the effects of these teachings? They
were so bad that Paul compares them to *gangrene*! Just a few
years after his first letter to Timothy, Paul includes Hymenaeus
again in his list of heretics who had infected the Ephesian
fellowship:

> But avoid irreverent, empty speech, for this will pro-
> duce an even greater measure of godlessness. And their
> word will spread like gangrene, among whom are
> Hymenaeus and Philetus. They have deviated from the
> truth, saying that the resurrection has already taken
> place, and are overturning the faith of some.
> (2 Tim. 2:16–18).

Alexander as well does not escape Paul's scathing recounting: "Alexander the coppersmith did great harm to me. The Lord

will repay him according to his works. Watch out for him yourself, because he strongly opposed our words" (2 Tim. 4:14–15).

What precisely were these church leaders doing that so infuriated Paul and damaged the church? If Paul's two letters to
Timothy are any indication, the Ephesian church had descended
into infighting, deception, heresy, and hatred. Among Paul's
accusations:

1. The church was always arguing, even during worship and
prayer. "Therefore I want the men in every place to pray, lifting
up holy hands without anger or argument" (1 Tim. 2:8).

2. The women were attending the worship services dressed
seductively, decked out as if they were going out on the town.
"Also, the women are to dress themselves in modest clothing,
with decency and good sense; not with elaborate hairstyles, gold,
pearls, or expensive apparel, but with good works, as is proper
for women who affirm that they worship God" (1 Tim. 2:9–10).

3. The leaders, pastors, and deacons were not measuring up
to the standards of God, so Paul had to explicitly delineate their
qualifications (1 Tim. 3:1–13).

4. Their behavior had so disintegrated that Paul rushed
the letter to them, so that, if he were delayed, they would
"know how people ought to act in God's household, which is the
church of the living God, the pillar and foundation of the truth"
(1 Tim. 3:15).

5. These false teachers were developing followings within the
church body, and members were taking sides. Paul resolutely
calls these types of acts demonic, and calls those leaders hypocrites. "Now the Spirit explicitly says that in the latter times
some will depart from the faith, paying attention to deceitful spirits and the teachings of demons, through the hypocrisy of liars
whose consciences are seared" (1 Tim. 4:1–2).

6. Evidently, these same leaders were mocking Timothy
behind his back, maligning his ability because of his age. "No one
should despise your youth; instead, you should be an example to
the believers in speech, in conduct, in love, in faith, in purity"
(1 Tim. 4:12).

7. Were these divisive leaders in the fellowship effective in silencing Pastor Timothy? Well, though they had not succeeded in removing him from leadership, they certainly had affected his demeanor. Paul had to continually remind Timothy to be strong. The battle was taking its toll on him. "For God has not given us a spirit of fearfulness, but one of power, love, and sound judgment" (2 Tim. 1:7).

8. These splinter leaders were spiritually poisonous. Paul reserves his most severe critique for them. "If anyone teaches other doctrine and does not agree with the sound teaching of our Lord Jesus Christ and with the teaching that promotes godliness, he is conceited, understanding nothing, but having a sick interest in disputes and arguments over words. From these come envy, quarreling, slanders, evil suspicions, and constant disagreement among men whose minds are depraved and deprived of the truth, who imagine that godliness is a way to material gain" (1 Tim. 6:3–5).

Were Paul's stern warnings to the church at Ephesus enough to wake them from their spiritual slumber and cause them to reclaim their church for Christ? Sadly, no. In Paul's second letter to Timothy, he tells him, "Charging them before God not to fight about words; this is in no way profitable and leads to the ruin of the hearers" (2 Tim. 2:14). In fact, he instructs Timothy, "But reject foolish and ignorant disputes, knowing that they breed quarrels. The Lord's slave must not quarrel, but must be gentle to everyone, able to teach, and patient, instructing his opponents with gentleness. Perhaps God will grant them repentance to know the truth. Then they may come to their senses and escape the Devil's trap, having been captured by him to do his will" (2 Tim. 2:23–26).

Can you relate to Paul's dilemma? Have you ever experienced such things in church? Here is one interesting point to emphasize to the church member who is upset by the fighting in his church: At the very end of Paul's final letter to Timothy, he sends his greetings to Priscilla and Aquila (2 Tim. 4:19). This faithful couple had remained loyal at Ephesus, through the splits, divisions, political machinations, and fights. For over a decade (from roughly AD 54–67) they continued in the Ephesian work in spite of the tragic condition in which they often found the fellowship. It can be done.

Perhaps the most distressing portion of this narrative is this: The Ephesian church apparently learned their lesson, but at a catastrophic price. When the apostle John wrote the words of the Lord to the church at Ephesus in Revelation 2:1–7, he commended them for resolving their problems with divisions and heresy. He states:

> I know your works, your labor, and your endurance, and that you cannot tolerate evil. You have tested those who call themselves apostles and are not, and you have found them to be liars. You also possess endurance and have tolerated [many things] because of My name, and have not grown weary. (Rev. 2:2–3)

Yet the price for this victory was dear. They affirmed orthodoxy at the cost of joy. The church at Ephesus was a mere shell of the joyous fellowship of their youth, some forty years prior to John's writing. Notice the Lord's warning: "But I have this against you: you have abandoned the love [you had] at first. Remember then how far you have fallen; repent, and do the works you did at first. Otherwise, I will come to you and remove your lampstand from its place—unless you repent" (Rev. 2:4–5).

The Ephesian church was a fellowship of extremes. They were schizophrenic. Either they were joyously seeing God do the miraculous (as in Acts 19:11–20), or arguing and fighting viciously (2 Tim. 2:14), or piously maintaining orthodoxy without joy or passion (Rev. 2:4–5). Tragic? Yes. Unique? No.

Corinth: A Chaotic and Lethal Fellowship

If Ephesus is a prime example of an unhealthy church, then Corinth must surely be the most notorious fellowship. Prior to Paul's arrival in Ephesus on his second missionary journey, Paul came to Corinth, a city linked to Greece by a four-mile stretch of land jutting out of the southern Peloponnesus islands. With two seaports (Cenchraea and Lechaeum) and a thriving economy, Corinth was the commercial center of Greece, even surpassing Athens.

Paul spent a significant portion of time in Corinth, establishing a strong church there. Crispus, the synagogue leader in Corinth, and his entire family came to faith in Jesus Christ, and many others followed, according to Acts 18:7–8. From their humble beginnings in the home of Titius Justus, the church at Corinth grew in number and devotion.

But when we examine Paul's two lengthy letters to the Corinthian church, we find a shattered and damaged fellowship. Indeed, the church at Corinth has become synonymous with wickedness and debauchery. Among Paul's indictments of this church, one finds an alarming litany of sin:

1. They were arguing, dividing, and taking sides (1 Cor. 1:10–17).

2. They were acting like infants (1 Cor. 3:1–9).

3. An active member had participated in an incestuous affair with his father's wife (1 Cor. 5:1–11).

4. Church members were taking one another to court (1 Cor. 6:1–6).

5. Marital wars had broken out in the church, affecting the fellowship (1 Cor. 7:1–19).

6. They were fighting over issues of food (1 Cor. 8:1–13).

7. Women within the fellowship were fighting as well (1 Cor. 11:3–15).

8. The agape love feast and the tangential Lord's Supper celebration had descended into chaos, catering to the rich, with members becoming drunk and people jumping in line and eating in front of the impoverished members (1 Cor. 11:17–22).

9. Due to the seriousness of these sins at the Lord's Table, many members were sick, and others had died (1 Cor. 11:30).

10. They were fighting over the superiority of their individual spiritual gifts (1 Cor. 12:1–31).

11. They were not united by love, but rather identified by fighting (1 Cor. 13:1–13).

12. Their services had become chaotic, with competing members attempting to speak in tongues (1 Cor. 14:1–40).

13. They were fighting over leadership and developing alliances against one another (1 Cor. 16:15–18).

Quite a poignant portrait of the Corinthian church! Paul's censure of Corinth contains some of his most explicit language. Did they turn from their sinful ways and consolidate under the lordship of Christ, as Paul had instructed?

In the interim between Paul's first and second letter to the church, they had evidently attempted to rectify the major problems. When Paul was in Macedonia, he greeted Titus, who brought the report of the Corinthian church's response to his letter. He recognized that they were hurt by the letter, but that was not his intent. He did not apologize for the effect of the letter on their fellowship, however, because Paul noted that it caused them sorrow and repentance (2 Cor. 7:5–12). In fact, Paul was:

made to rejoice even more over the joy Titus had,
because his spirit was refreshed by all of you. For if
I have made any boast to him about you, I have not
been embarrassed; but as I have spoken everything to
you in truth, so our boasting to Titus has also turned out
to be the truth. And his affection toward you is even
greater as he remembers the obedience of all of you, and
how you received him with fear and trembling. I rejoice
that I have complete confidence in you. (2 Cor. 7:13–16)

Unfortunately, all of the problems were not resolved by Paul's rebuke. Even though the leaders of the church were broken by Paul's words, they were also sullen and resentful, withholding their hearts from Paul (2 Cor. 6:11–13). In fact, some of the members had responded to the letter by attacking Paul personally: "For it is said, 'His letters are weighty and powerful, but his physical presence is weak, and his public speaking is despicable'" (2 Cor. 10:10).

Who was leading this revolt against Paul? Who was continuing the church's open defiance against holiness and godliness? A subset of shadow leaders within the church who conspired to pull the church at Corinth out of Paul's grasp. These divisive leaders were setting themselves in opposition to Paul and were presenting themselves as the rightful alternative to Paul's perceived nagging. Paul did not shrink from their challenge. He even mocked them:

But I fear that, as the serpent deceived Eve by his cunning, your minds may be corrupted from a complete and pure devotion to Christ. For if a person comes and preaches another Jesus, whom we did not preach, or you receive a different spirit, which you had not received, or a different gospel, which you had not accepted, you put up with it splendidly! Now I consider myself in no way inferior to the "super-apostles." Though untrained in public speaking, I am certainly not [untrained] in knowledge. Indeed, we have always made that clear to you in everything. (2 Cor. 11:3–6)

In short, Paul feared that though Corinth was openly remorseful concerning his charges, they were secretly unrepentant and defiant. The church at Corinth, Paul believed, was a seething cauldron of chaos, and it was only a matter of time before they showed their true colors:

For I fear that perhaps when I come I will not find you to be what I want, and I may not be found by you to be what you want; there may be quarreling, jealousy, outbursts of anger, selfish ambitions, slander, gossip, arrogance, and disorder. I fear that when I come my God will again humiliate me in your presence, and I will grieve for many who sinned before and have not repented of the uncleanness, sexual immorality, and promiscuity they practiced. (2 Cor. 12:20–21)

To put a measure of finality to his charge, Paul closes his letter by urging the members of the fellowship to examine their salvation. The implication was clear—Paul was not sure that the people to whom he was writing, this fellowship of chaos, were even saved (2 Cor. 13:5).

What Is Wrong with These People?

Many of you have been reading the narratives of the churches at Ephesus and Corinth and have been nodding, recognizing trends you see every Sunday. You have silently wondered how the churches with which you are familiar have descended into such a state. You have watched in disbelief as fellow Christians, supposedly brothers and sisters in Christ, have destroyed one another, even while standing in the church itself. You have seen similarities between the leadership in your local churches and the examples at Ephesus and Corinth.

And you have silently wondered: *What is wrong with these people? How did they ever get like this? Do they not recognize how they are acting? Can they not see that?*

The answer is a bit more complicated than a mere changing of the mind; there must be a changing of the heart. A heart change demands true repentance. True repentance demands an actual diagnosis of the root problem—sin. Sin, in all of its manifestations, is a poison and a disease. That is where this book comes in.

Caveats: The Purpose of This Book

If in fact the church of the living God is a *body* as Paul describes it, and if in fact churches are dying and injured, perhaps the best way to study these things is to see the major problems in the church ailments. Spiritual diseases. Lethal poisons in the body of Christ. These diseases are often pathologies, and sometimes they are toxins. Scripture contains examples of men and women who were *venomous*. Like carnivorous animals, they prey on helpless and trusting sheep. They destroy the flock. The lives of these biblical characters are not to be emulated as good examples, but they should be studied intently.

Toxins

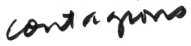

Why? Because their descendants are still in our churches. They are still carriers of these deadly diseases, and perhaps worst of all, they are highly contagious. Each of these maladies can be deadly if left untreated. Unless we are prepared to deal with them, they will rise to the level of an epidemic. To cure the disease, one must first understand the symptoms.

Please understand this caveat: The descriptions of spiritual problems given in this book do not in any way diminish the seriousness of the actual *physical* maladies. As pastors we have dealt too often with the painful effects of these serious diseases, pathologies, and psychoses. Indeed, it is our hope that this work might even amplify the serious nature of these diseases by illustrating the spiritual dimension and effects each of these ailments may have. Many of these issues are psychological, but in the spiritual realm, all of these are poisonous and cancerous.

The difference between those afflicted with a spiritual malady and the physical equivalent is that the spiritual disease always involves a choice. Many who suffer from variant forms of cancer inherited them genetically; they did not have a choice. However, each person who is infected by a spiritual disease has the choice to be cured. It is a matter of the will, not genetics. They are not victims; they are perpetrators.

The purpose of this book is to expose the diseases, poisons, and ailments found in almost epidemic proportions in virtually every church. We shall examine the symptoms, diagnose a cure, and give a biblical prognosis. The impact of these afflictions is profound. They kill countless churches every year. They destroy friendships among believers. They cause irreparable damage to the witness of Christ to a dying and skeptical world. These diseases can spread quickly through a church. Without a cure, they are almost always terminal. Rather than waiting until the death of a church, fellowship, or friendship, and performing an autopsy, we believe it would be better to diagnose the problem while the church still has a chance of recovery.

The encouraging news is that unless your church has "flatlined," there is still hope. Christ can rescue your church. It is wrong simply to lament the onset of the symptoms and the disease. We must also seek a cure.

> *Every church has three animals in the flock: sheep, goats and wolves.*
> *The job of biblical leadership is simple:*
> *Love the sheep.*
> *Convert the goats.*
> *Kill the wolves.*
>
> —Anonymous

Chapter 2

Atrophy: Shrunken Faith and Coasting on the Past

Isaac and Second Hand Victories
Genesis 21–27

As brutal as the following story seems, it actually took place.

Steve was your prototypical modern pastor. We have changed his name to protect the guilty, but suffice it to say that you have probably met many "Steves" in your past.

As a young preacher, Steve had quickly climbed to the top of the denominational ladder. As a seminary student, he had taken a small country church in Texas and had seen it grow tremendously. His energy, vigor, and faithfulness to the task of preaching and pastoring had built him quite a reputation.

Following his graduation from seminary, Steve had his choice of churches that were clamoring for his leadership. As a result, Steve moved nine times in twenty years. In every instance, he became the pastor of a larger church. Each move brought him closer and closer to his dream of a megachurch, with thousands of people in attendance and all the amenities that went along with it.

Please do not assume that Steve was just a stereotypical "climber" who had no spiritual inclinations. Indeed, in his earliest pastorates, Steve had genuinely desired to see God move among the people he served. Revivals, special services, and innovative ideas certainly bespoke his desire. It is just that in each ensuing move, it became easier for Steve to "coast." Many of the sermons that had inspired the people in his earlier churches began to creep into his new churches. Methods that had seemed innovative and fresh when Steve first implemented them in those smaller congregations began to become "old hat" to him now. At times, Steve's wife and children worried that he was on "autopilot," cruising along with methods and messages he could do in his sleep.

Added to this pattern was the fact that no pastor can establish lasting relationships in just two years, which was the average of his pastoral tenures. Just as soon as Steve's family had begun to form friendships in an area, the family was moving again to take a larger church. Once, in a moment of frustration, Steve's wife muttered that the most lasting relationship she had established was with the moving company!

At the age of forty-five, Steve was poised to achieve his dream. A ministerial friend had recommended him to one of the largest churches in a neighboring state. Along with the glowing reviews of his seminary friends, Steve felt he was certain to be called. To ensure he had a final recommendation, Steve called on a prominent pastor who had served as a mentor in Steve's early years. This minister was universally beloved, and his recommendation would move Steve to the top of the search committee's list.

Placing a phone call on a bright Monday morning, Steve cheerily greeted his pastor-mentor with the news that the committee from the well-known church was going to be calling for a recommendation.

"Of course, you are my first reference," Steve said, "because you have known me for the longest period of time."

During the opening pleasantries, Steve casually mentioned the attendance at his present church and the various denominational positions to which he had been appointed recently. "It seems that after twenty years of pastoring," Steve concluded, "I am about to enter the big leagues, like you. Are you ready for the phone call?"

Steve was a bit bewildered at the silence that followed his last sentence. *It was more than just a pause,* he thought. It was a pregnant pause, which often came when a person was thinking of the right words to say something difficult. Why was his hero taking so long to answer? Was this man's advanced age finally catching up to him?

Finally, after what seemed like an eternity to Steve, his mentor spoke slowly, with the words coming with the strength of a resolve that must have been building for some time.

"Steve," he began, "I love you like a son, so this is not easy for me."

Steve sat in stunned silence as he sensed a rebuke coming.

"But I cannot recommend you to this church. I have heard the same rumors about your name being in consideration there, and I knew the time would come when you would ask me to recommend you, but I cannot."

Steve thought for a minute, and then spoke.

"Is there something wrong with the church?" he asked quizzically. Steve had heard that churches of this size could often be cauldrons of impious leadership. "Is the church much too big for its own good? Does it have big problems?"

"No," the pastor said slowly. "It is not too big. In fact, it is one of the best churches I know. The fact is, Steve, that you are too small for the church. I hate to say this, but you are not ready for this church."

Steve could not believe what he was hearing. *Not ready?* He had been preparing for this move his entire life!

Finally, through a whirlwind of hurt feelings, Steve blurted out a response.

"Pastor, I cannot believe you think I am not ready. I have been pastoring for twenty years."

Before Steve could finish his thought, the pastor interrupted him.

"No, Steve, you haven't," he said gently. "You haven't pastored for twenty years. You have pastured for two years, *ten times.*"

The wise elder paused to let the words sink in.

"You have never established yourself anywhere, Steve. Every time a bigger opportunity comes along, your ambition gets the best of you, and you jump. Consequently, you have never really built anything. You always come to a location where another man has poured himself into the work. You are like the guy who sits on the bench an entire basketball game, and then comes in during the final two minutes, makes one or two passes, and then screams, 'We won!' You didn't win anything. You have coasted for twenty years on other men's sweat and labor."

Steve sat at his desk, shocked and numb. Feebly, he asked, "How can you say that, Pastor?" He felt all of his aspirations and dreams slipping away, and a cold, gnawing pain developing in the pit of his stomach.

"Son," the senior pastor said slowly, "you are preaching the same sermons now that you were preaching fifteen years ago. The only things that have changed are the illustrations. You are doing the same programs, making the same points, and following the same protocols that you did when we served in neighboring churches so many years ago.

"This church would eat you alive if you went there," the pastor continued. "Your spiritual muscles haven't been tested in over a decade, and you just can't coast in a church like this. You have to be ready for such a challenge, and you just are not.

"As soon as a problem arises at this church, you will do what you always do—begin to look for a bigger and better thing. The sad thing is, there is no 'bigger and better' thing than this church. You will become frustrated and overwhelmed. You have coasted on your talents for too long, and you have allowed your abilities as a natural speaker and leader to get in the way of true, God-sent victories."

Steve sat still and silent, with the phone barely touching his ear. Tears trickled down his cheek as he muttered a hollow benediction to the phone call, and he weakly hung up the receiver. At first, his natural instinct was to react with anger. Surely this man had betrayed him. Surely he had a right to cross him off his references and chalk it up to senility.

But Steve knew better. This elder statesman knew Steve better than anyone, except perhaps his wife. In recent days, Steve had even grown suspicious of his wife's leanings as well. She would quietly roll her eyes whenever he spoke forcefully from the pulpit about a "new" sermon series, knowing that it had been in "rotation" for a decade. Perhaps she felt the same as this pastor. Perhaps his entire family knew.

Slowly, the realization came over Steve like a bad case of the flu—he was suffering from the Isaac Syndrome. Steve was coasting on yesterday's victories. He had not tried anything new or fresh in years. He was suffering from spiritual atrophy, and he knew it, deep within his heart.

Spiritual atrophy—the deterioration of your spiritual muscles from lack of use—is such an insidious disease and poison that it afflicts virtually every Christian at one time or another. Resting on our laurels and rejoicing in victories long since fought is so winsome that entire churches have been built on this disease! They have become mausoleums to yesterday and museums to display revivals long ago, rather than sacred places where men and women seek the face of God daily.

Like the Israelites, Christians learn that manna which was fresh and nutritious yesterday becomes moldy today. Each and every day must be marked by a fresh confrontation with the Lord. The sad fact, however, is that moldy manna is an acquired taste for too many of us. We become complacent in our daily walk with God. Muscles that at one time were pulsing with power have withered toward atrophy. We no longer have the muscles we once had. We become a shadow of our former selves.

Spiritual atrophy is perhaps the most prevalent spiritual disease in modern Christianity. It is marked by Christians who have had a glorious past, walking with God, serving God, but who have stopped seeking him, stopped serving him, and now, their abilities, discernment, and wisdom have lessened. Our spiritual "muscles" must be exercised and tested every day. Without such rigorous engagement, we wither.

The "poster child" for spiritual atrophy is the Hebrew patriarch Isaac. If ever there was a man who left all of his God-given potential unrealized, it was Isaac. He was the proverbial man of God who "was born on third base, but thought he had hit a triple."

Case Study of Atrophy: Isaac and the Silver Spoon

It may seem odd to the reader to examine Isaac in such a harsh light. Isn't he listed in the litany of God's covenant promises throughout the Bible? Thirty-three times in Scripture, the grandfather, father, and son combination of "Abraham, Isaac, and Jacob" is mentioned, beginning with Jacob's own realization of the covenant linkage in Genesis 32:9–12:

Then Jacob said, "God of my father Abraham and God of my father Isaac, the LORD who said to me, 'Go back to your land and to your family, and I will cause you to prosper,' I am unworthy of all the kindness and faithfulness You have shown Your servant. Indeed, I crossed over this Jordan with my staff, and now I have become two camps. Please rescue me from the hand of my brother Esau, for I am afraid of him; otherwise, he may come and attack me, the mothers, and their children. You have said, 'I will cause you to prosper, and I will make your offspring like the sand of the sea, which cannot be counted.'"

In fact, even Stephen notes the correlation in his final sermon before his death, in Acts 7:32. Isaac is mentioned 119 times in the

Bible, but almost always in relation to either his father Abraham, or his progeny, Jacob and Joseph.

Read the preceding sentence again, and ask yourself this question:

What exactly did Isaac ever do?

All of his pedigree, all of his training, and all of his preparation went into a life that could have been an amazing walk with God—but again, what exactly did he do? He inherited everything he ever had, and certainly he was part of the direct lineage of the twelve tribes. But any cursory reading of the Old Testament will show that Isaac was the weakest of the four generations. He never directly claimed his mantle or took hold of his own blessing. In marking the book of Genesis, one sees that Abraham is the main actor in Genesis 12–24, Jacob is the main actor in Genesis 28–35, and Joseph is the protagonist of Genesis 37–50. Isaac claims only three chapters of the biblical narrative, and even then his weakness becomes our greatest lesson.

Your Greatest Days Are in the Past (Gen. 21–22)

One of the distinguishing marks of spiritual atrophy is that your greatest days of blessing are in your distant past. The birth of Isaac, promised in the Abrahamic covenant of Genesis 12:1–3, comes to fruition in Genesis 21:1–8. His birth was greeted with a great celebration and joy in Genesis 21:6–8: "Sarah said, 'God has made me laugh, and everyone who hears will laugh with me.' She also said, 'Who would have told Abraham that Sarah would nurse children? Yet I have borne him a son in his old age.' The child grew and was weaned, and Abraham held a great feast on the day Isaac was weaned."

Even Isaac's name, meaning "laughter," bespoke a celebration of God's blessing. Surely his life would exemplify God's riches and favor.

Yet the next step in Isaac's life illustrates his most profound example—that of a sacrifice. Told by God to take his son to the top of Mount Moriah, Abraham led the youthful Isaac to the mountain to give an offering to the Lord. Notice the words of God as he called Abraham to this test of faith. They put the birth of his first son, Ishmael, in perspective, as the covenant is clearly seen in Isaac: "Take your son," He said, "your only [son] Isaac, whom you love, go to the land of Moriah, and offer him there as a burnt offering on one of the mountains I will tell you about" (Gen. 22:2).

During the journey, Isaac uttered his only words, which show both the intense struggle of Abraham and God's imminent provision. Genesis 22:6–8 says:

Abraham took the wood for the burnt offering and laid it on his son Isaac. In his hand he took the fire and the sacrificial knife, and the two of them walked on together. Then Isaac spoke to his father Abraham and said, "My father." And he replied, "Here I am, my son." Isaac said, "The fire and the wood are here, but where is the lamb for the burnt offering?" Abraham answered, "God Himself will provide the lamb for the burnt offering, my son." Then the two of them walked on together.

Even in this, his shining moment, Isaac is seen as an unknowing participant in his harbinger of the sacrifice of Christ on the cross. Isaac totally depends on his father. This is not a bad thing, in and of itself, but it is telling when examining the life of Isaac. Even as God provides a substitute, Isaac is spared, and Abraham is the one whose faith was tested.

You Depend on Others to Provide the Blessing (Gen. 24)

Abraham set about to get his forty-year-old son Isaac a wife. As Abraham's servant finds Rebekah by the well (Gen. 24:1–8, 15–26), Isaac is found meditating in the fields (24:63–67). Even in his adulthood, Isaac was dependent on his father to provide the blessing for him. Sound familiar? Many Christians come to church, expecting the pastor or Bible study leader to "spoon-feed" them, even though they are capable of seeking God's will themselves. Any pastor who has received a midnight phone call can speak to this issue!

Your Discernment Withers and You Become Easily Entangled (Gen. 25–26)

The life of Isaac is marked by his lessening spiritual thrust. He fell into the same sin of lying like his father, even though he should have known better. Compare Abraham's lie in Genesis 20:2 and Isaac's lie in Genesis 26:7. Both father and son tried to pass off their wives as their sisters. Expedience was Isaac's motivation. He seemed to dwell in the land of "if it works, do it." His labor, though certainly blessed of God, was also adherence of another man's blessing. He is seen digging up his father's wells in Genesis 26:13–15, and then again in 26:16–18. He seems content not to stake his claim, but to remain safely within his father's parameters.

You Are Driven by Your Appetites (Gen. 25–27)

The sad conclusion of a life of atrophy is compulsiveness. Isaac was a man driven by his appetites. We first see this clearly when Moses writes that Isaac loved his son Esau because of his love for meat. After the birth of their twins, the family was divided along the lines drawn by Isaac's incessant love for temporal pleasure over and beyond any spiritual consideration. "When the boys grew up, Esau became an expert hunter, an outdoorsman, but Jacob was a quiet man who stayed at home. Isaac loved Esau *because he had a taste for wild game,* but Rebekah loved Jacob" (Gen. 25:27–28).

In fact, Isaac's compulsive love for the satisfaction of his temporal needs led to his worst heartache—his deception by Jacob and his mother in Genesis 27. Though it can be said that Jacob and Rebekah were responsible for the deception and sin, Isaac bore some of the responsibility as well. Obsessed with his need for one final meal of venison on his deathbed, Isaac displayed no discernment and was easily betrayed.

The Ravages of Atrophy: The Stolen Blessing (Gen. 27)

The tragic end to the story further reveals the depths to which Isaac had fallen. Though we often preach this event in the lives of the Israelites focused on Jacob, Esau, and their mother, consider for a moment Isaac's actions.

As he lay dying, Isaac's final thoughts were not on his legacy or the future of his children and wife but on his stomach.

When Isaac was old and his eyes were so weak that he could not see, he called his older son Esau and said to him, "My son." And he answered, "Here I am." He said, "Look, I am old and do not know the day of my death. Take your [hunting] gear, your quiver and bow, and go out in the field to hunt some game for me. Then make me the delicious food that I love and bring it to me to eat, so that I can bless you before I die." (Gen. 27:1–4)

Those around him knew that his weakness would be their fortune. Isaac's wife, Rebekah, convinced Jacob to work the ruse, using the food to trick Isaac into giving Jacob his blessing (Gen. 27:5–17).

Isaac's discernment had withered, along with his strength. Isaac knew that hunting would take some time, but as quickly as Jacob could find the tools of his deception, he rushed in and dissuaded Isaac's objections by lying and attributing his sin to a miracle of God. Then, though Isaac thought he heard the voice of his son Jacob, he was convinced it was Esau, due to the goatskin Jacob had placed on his arm (Gen. 27:18–24).

Regardless of his doubts or hesitations, Isaac quickly turned his attention to the driving force in his life: his appetite. "Then he said, 'Serve me, and let me eat some of my son's game so that I can bless you.' Jacob brought it to him, and he ate; he brought him wine, and he drank" (Gen. 27:25).

With his appetite satisfied, Isaac gave Jacob the blessing and the inheritance. Once Esau discovered the fraud, he alerted his father. Isaac's response is quite telling: "Isaac began to tremble uncontrollably. 'Who was it then,' he said, 'who hunted game and brought it to me? I ate it all before you came in, and I blessed him. Indeed, he will be blessed!'" (Gen. 27:33).

Can you imagine what was going through Isaac's mind? Was he wondering how he could have been fooled? Was he questioning his weakened judgment in his final hours? It does not seem so. Instead, Isaac trembled violently with anger. *How could they do this to me? I am a victim!*

One would assume that a believer, being made aware of his weakness, would repent and attempt to right the wrong. Not Isaac. Instead, he resigned himself to his state and informed Esau that nothing could be done. He had grown accustomed to his weakness, and Esau would suffer the consequences.

Case Studies: Noah and Elijah

Other case studies of spiritual atrophy also reveal the insidious nature of this disease. Though Noah showed exemplary faith in Genesis 6–9, and he survived the universal Flood along with his wife, sons, and daughters-in-law, we read a tragic epitaph on such a great life in Genesis 9:28–29: "Now Noah lived 350 years after the flood. So Noah's life lasted 950 years; then he died."

Three hundred and fifty years without a single report of godliness! In fact, after the Flood, the Bible records Noah's descent into drunkenness, carousing, and cursing (Gen. 9:20–27). This is certainly not an illustration of finishing well.

Another similar story is that of Elisha. Can the case be made that he simply wanted to ride Elijah's victories himself? The evidence seems to support another conclusion—that Elisha was willing to pay the price and serve the Lord in order to build upon Elijah's ministry, rather than lethargically coasting.

> Elijah left there and found Elisha son of Shaphat as he was plowing. Twelve teams of oxen were in front of him, and he was with the twelfth team. Elijah walked by him and threw his mantle over him. Elisha left the oxen, ran to follow Elijah, and said, "Please let me kiss

my father and mother, and then I will follow you." "Go
on back," he replied, "for what have I done to you?" So
he turned back from following him, took the team of
oxen, and slaughtered them. With the oxen's wooden
yoke and plow, he cooked the meat and gave it to the
people, and they ate. Then he left, followed Elijah, and
served him. (1 Kings 19:19–21)

Elisha illustrates his desire to serve God totally by burning
the equipment of his former life. Serving the Lord together, each
man understood they had a singular service to offer God. When
Elijah was ready to be transported to heaven on the chariot of fire,
Elisha discovered that the mantle of God was not an easy life.
Even Elijah himself reiterated the difficulty in 2 Kings 2:9–10, 15:

After they had crossed over, Elijah said to Elisha, "Tell
[me] what I can do for you before I am taken from
you." So Elisha answered, "Please, let there be a double
portion of your spirit on me." Elijah replied, "You have
asked for something difficult. If you see me being taken
from you, you will have it. If not, you won't." When the
sons of the prophets from Jericho, who were facing
him, saw him, they said, "The spirit of Elijah rests on
Elisha."

This does not seem to be a man committed to an easy path or
second-hand blessings.

The central point of the distinction between Elisha and Isaac
is simple: Building on a previous victory or generation is blessed.
However, coasting on previous victories is a sin. It leads to a
weakened faith and withered spiritual muscles. It is atrophy.

Caleb's Cure for Spiritual Atrophy (Josh. 14:6–14)

Though Caleb was a faithful servant of the Lord throughout
his life, we believe his greatest legacy was seen in his last years.
After the Israelites had been led into the Promised Land after a
forty-year sojourn in the desert, there was intense rejoicing. It
must have also been a time of immense relief for Caleb. This elder

statesman of Israel finally lived in the land he had surveyed so many years ago. Certainly, he would rest in retirement here, satisfied that he had finished his journey and been found faithful.

Nothing could be further from the truth. With an emboldened faith and a forward gaze, Caleb surpassed the embryonic faith of the young husbands and fathers who stood gathered before Joshua. This grandfather now spoke, and he must have shocked all those who heard his words:

The descendants of Judah approached Joshua at Gilgal, and Caleb son of Jephunneh the Kenizzite said to him, "You know what the LORD promised Moses the man of God at Kadesh-barnea about you and me. I was 40 years old when Moses the LORD's servant sent me from Kadesh-barnea to scout the land, and I brought back an honest report. My brothers who went with me caused the people's hearts to melt with fear, but I remained loyal to the LORD my God. On that day Moses promised me, 'The land where you have set foot will be an inheritance for you and your descendants forever, because you have remained loyal to the LORD my God.' As you see, the LORD has kept me alive [these] 45 years as He promised, since the LORD spoke this word to Moses while Israel was journeying in the wilderness. Here I am today, 85 years old. I am still as strong today as I was the day Moses sent me out. My strength for battle and for daily tasks is now as it was then. *Now give me this hill country the LORD promised [me] on that day,* because you heard then that the Anakim are there, as well as large fortified cities. Perhaps the LORD will be with me and I will drive them out as the LORD promised" (Josh. 14:6–12).

Caleb did not ask for a rocking chair or a retirement home. He did not ask that they dedicate a stained glass window in his honor. He did not ask for his own parking space near the tabernacle entrance. Caleb looked forward and asked for a new challenge.

✗ Caleb knew the secret of a vibrant faith is a daily faith. He did not remind the Israelites of his prior service. He simply faced the future and asked to continue serving him. Did God call Caleb to do such a thing, or was he simply a deluded old man with dreams beyond his capacity? See for yourself in the following verses: "Then Joshua blessed Caleb son of Jephunneh and gave him Hebron as an inheritance. Therefore, Hebron has belonged to Caleb son of Jephunneh the Kenizzite as an inheritance to this day, because he remained loyal to the LORD, the God of Israel" (Josh. 14:13–14).

God blessed the land in perpetuity because Caleb did not just start in faithfulness; he remained faithful. As long as there was breath in Caleb's body, he had work to do. So do you.

Do you recognize anyone with spiritual atrophy? A child of God whose greatest days are far behind him? A Sunday school teacher who has stopped teaching? A choir member who has retired from singing? A Christian who is coasting on blessings and miracles that were won long ago? The truth is that all of us are in danger of spiritual atrophy. Ask yourself, When was the last time I claimed God's promise for a new task? Not for an answer to some prayer for someone else. Not for an answer to a financial or physical need. But a task that will take labor and study and work and the blessing of God to accomplish it.

This type of reconditioning does not come easily. Your spiritual muscles will ache once again. You will feel the burden of time constraints, pressing needs, and deadlines. Yet you will also notice that you will feel alive again! You will sense God's special enablement, which you long ago may have lost. It will feel hard, but it will feel good. And the ungodly alternative is not a winsome one. It involves moldy manna.

Moldy Manna and Daily Devotion

Neither Isaac nor Noah lived to see themselves rectify their spiritual apathy. The cure was in a life of direction, not reflection. ✗ God never blesses the past without pressing us to the future.

Look at the Israelites. The Lord, having brought them out of the slavery of Egypt, did not leave them without provision. Exodus 16 tells us of his care for his children, but also includes an ominous warning.

This is what the LORD has commanded: "Gather as much of it as each person needs to eat. You may take two quarts per individual, according to the number of people each of you has in his tent." So the Israelites did this. Some gathered a lot, some a little. When they measured it by quarts, the person who gathered a lot had no surplus, and the person who gathered a little had no shortage. Each gathered as much as he needed to eat. Moses said to them, "No one is to let any of it remain until morning." But they didn't listen to Moses; some people left part of it until morning, and it bred worms and smelled. Therefore Moses was angry with them. They gathered it every morning. Each gathered as much as he needed to eat, but when the sun grew hot, it melted. (Exod. 16:16–21)

The provision of God and the blessing of God came with a fundamental condition: the children of Israel had to gather manna *daily*.

They could not coast on victories won a week before, or even a day before. Illustrative of God's method was the condition of yesterday's manna: it was moldy, worm-infested, and putrid.

So is coasting on past victories.

If you assume that you have served God enough in the past, and that God is satisfied with your previous service, then please read that paragraph again. If the Israelites dared to try to store up the manna, it would become diseased and infested. God wanted them to seek him and serve him *daily*.

If that illustration alone does not convince you to get off the padded pew and once again join God's coalition of the willing, then search the New Testament and see to what degree we are to live in the daily tense:

- Jesus reminded us to thank God for our *daily* bread (Matt. 6:11).

- We are to deny ourselves, take up our cross *daily*, and follow (Luke 9:23).
- The Bereans were blessed because they searched the Scriptures *daily* (Acts 17:11).
- Paul noted that in Christ, we die *daily* (1 Cor. 15:31).

Daily bread. Daily prayer. Daily study. Daily death. It does not sound as if God is satisfied with our past victories, or that he blesses us when we coast.

Perhaps we can now understand the apostle Paul in a new light. This man of God, the unceasing missionary of the early church, was certainly a strong student of Scripture and a symbol of Christian maturity. So then why did he tell the Philippian church that he was still working toward a goal? Surely, if anyone had arrived, it would be Paul. Certainly if anyone deserved to retire and rest on a pew, it would be this incessant servant of God. Yet look at his testimony:

Not that I have already reached [the goal] or am already fully mature, but I make every effort to take hold of it because I also have been taken hold of by Christ Jesus. Brothers, I do not consider myself to have taken hold of it. But one thing I do: forgetting what is behind and reaching forward to what is ahead, I pursue as my goal the prize promised by God's heavenly call in Christ Jesus. Therefore, all who are mature should think this way. And if you think differently about anything, God will reveal this to you also. (Phil. 3:12–15)

Was Paul insisting that the only mature Christians are those who forget their past and continue to serve Christ? Would he not be satisfied if we just attended but never participated? The writer of Hebrews seems to suggest that coasting and not serving God daily has a devastating side effect—sin. More specifically, he warns that if we choose to retire, quit, or otherwise cease serving God, we are hardening our hearts in rebellion. God, he indicates, is always calling us to worship him through service.

Watch out, brothers, so that there won't be in any of you an evil, unbelieving heart that departs from the living God. But encourage each other daily, while it is still called today, so that none of you is hardened by sin's deception. For we have become companions of the Messiah if we hold firmly until the end the reality that we had at the start. As it is said: "Today, if you hear His voice, do not harden your hearts as in the rebellion." (Heb. 3:12–15)

These familiar words were not directed to the lost person who has not accepted Christ as Lord. These words were pointed at those who know God ("brothers"). The only conclusion is this: When we cease to serve him, we harden our hearts. When we harden our hearts, we have bought sin's deception. When we buy into the deception of sin, we are in active rebellion—rebellion against the Lord who calls us to serve him daily.

Chapter 3

Glossolitis: Swollen Tongues of Fire

Murmuring Miriam and Sowing Seeds of Discord
Numbers 12:1–15

It was Ergun's first Wednesday night prayer meeting at his new church. It was supposed to be part of the "honeymoon" period. Instead, it turned out to be a nightmare.

Walking into the sanctuary of that small country church, Ergun felt like he was in a dream. It was his first full-time church, complete with a parsonage. In a town with a population of 115, the pastor would obviously be a central character. Ergun hoped and prayed that he was up to the challenge. In the three days since the church had voted, the new pastor had read everything he could find on country living. Being an urbanite and having never even had a lawn, Ergun wrongly assumed that he could read up on farming and be ready. But nothing could have prepared him for what happened.

He felt taking a smaller church would be easier. The fact that he had received a unanimous vote also buoyed his assumptions. Of course, it was not difficult to receive a unanimous vote from seventeen people, but he did not allow that to dissuade him. He walked confidently down the central aisle, to the back room off the sanctuary, to get the marker board.

The church had the tradition of writing the prayer requests on the huge, five-foot-wide marker board. As members would share their requests, the pastor would write them down. The Wednesday night service was usually divided, half an hour for requests and prayer, and then a twenty-minute Bible lesson by the pastor. This night, the entire hour would be dedicated to the prayer meeting. Or rather, it would be dedicated to the fight stemming from the prayer meeting.

The requests began slowly. A case of gout here, a cousin with rheumatism there. The board was filled somewhat quickly with requests of varying seriousness. Some were heartbreaking, such as a broken home. Some were less serious, such as a mother asking for prayer for her fighting teenage sons. However, time seemed to stop when Doreen stood to share her request.

"Preacher," she began, "I am asking the church to pray for a woman in serious condition. She really needs our prayers."

Doreen then proceeded to share one of the most horrific stories Ergun had ever heard. This woman for whom Doreen was asking prayer had a serious condition that demanded a prolonged brain surgery. That afternoon, Doreen had heard the doctors say it was possible that the woman could die, even post-operatively, due to the extensive complications. By the time Doreen finished the report, the sanctuary was silent, except for the sound of Ergun writing the name of the woman on the marker board.

The darkest part of the tale, however, was yet to come. Doreen remained standing and spoke with a faltering voice. The elderly woman seemed almost broken over the tragedy. She continued to share that the woman's own husband chose her pre-operative moments to tell her that he was leaving her for another woman. The man was heartless and godless, she exclaimed.

The new pastor was in shock. He stood silently, unable to speak or even offer comfort.

The silence was broken by a solitary voice from the back. Another elderly woman, with hair the color of woven wool, spoke up with a brutal voice.

"Doreen, sit down and shut up!"

The pastor was aghast. He was unaccustomed to such a scathing rebuke in God's house. He assumed the woman in the back was a friend of the heartless husband. He was standing in the midst of a real-life, familial Shakespearean tragedy.

"Ma'am," Ergun began, "please let her finish her prayer request. I would ask that we don't speak to each other in that manner." He tried to summon all the courage he had to face down this conflict.

Doreen continued to share the unfolding horror this woman was facing. Doreen spoke of the woman's children and compounding debt. The depth of this woman's misfortune was almost unimaginable. The young preacher made a mental note to go to the hospital on Thursday morning, even skipping a seminary class. This was certainly more important.

Before Doreen could complete her thought, the white-haired woman in the back spoke up again.

"Doreen, would you *please* shut up? If you don't sit down and be quiet, I'm gonna come up there and punch you in the mouth!"

Now the pastor was simmering with rage. How dare this woman defend such a man? And how could she dare speak in such a manner in the church, threatening violence? Two older women fighting? What kind of horror had he inherited?

The new preacher scanned the approximately fifteen people in the church. Did anyone have a clue about what the preacher should do? The four men in the sanctuary, sitting with their wives, were looking down at their shoes. The other women were alternating looks between Doreen and the other women, as if they were watching gleefully as a fight unfolded. *This is too lurid for words,* the young preacher thought.

Finally he spoke. "Ma'am, I am not going to ask you again. Please do not interrupt a prayer request. This is a sacred place, and I believe such fighting is an ungodly show of . . ."

Before the new pastor could finish, the woman in the back stood up and yelled, "Preacher, that's my sister standin' in front of you, and that ain't a real woman, and it ain't a real husband, and it ain't a real surgery. She is sharin' a prayer request from her *soap opera* she saw this afternoon!"

So much for an auspicious beginning for a new pastor.

Spiritual Glossolitis:
The Swollen Tongue of the Saints

Glossolitis is a serious medical condition that is marked by a swelling of the tongue. In biblical terms, glossolitis occurs when the tongue is overused. It is, in our estimation, the most prevalent disease in the body of Christ and has the potential to destroy every church it infects. Gossip, in all of its sinister manifestations, is such a menacing threat that it has become epidemic. To make this plague worse, Christians have grown accustomed to its ravages. We assume that it "comes with the territory." This assumption is our greatest peril.

It has been said that, in the two decades since the outbreak of AIDS and AIDS-related diseases in Africa, some African villages have grown used to its lethal effects. An entire generation of children in these villages has been raised with the horrors of AIDS as a customary by-product of life. Where at one time it was viewed as the enemy, it is now part of the backdrop. It has always been there, as far as they know. Gossip has assumed the same position. Tragically, Christians have grown accustomed to the presence of gossip in our midst. It has become a befriended disease.

Ergun would learn to hesitate before recognizing Doreen to share any "prayer requests." Following the lead of the church members (even her vituperative sister), the young pastor began to understand that Doreen did not so much as share prayer requests, as she shared whatever juicy detail she had heard that week. No one was immune to Doreen's withering scrutiny: neighbors, relatives, even the pastor. She was obsessed with knowing the most exacting details about the lives around her. Whatever she could not gather, she often invented, filling in the gaps of knowledge.

She would stop the preacher boy in the hallway to whisper some obscure morsel from the community. It was always under the pretense of noting, "We really need to pray about this." She would glance around, conspiratorially, as if sharing a nuclear test code. Her whispers were covered with a cupped hand, and she would beckon the pastor to bring his ear near.

Ergun often wondered, *How does Doreen know so much?* Her gossip, like most gossip, contained just enough kernels of truth for validation, even if her details were not always syncopated with the truth. Yet she still *knew* so much. How was this possible?

The young preacher soon discovered that other members of the community were also privileged to get information that he never got. Was he somehow "out of the loop"? He would hear of an illness or accident, jump in his car, and race to the person's house, only to find twenty townspeople already gathered in the living room with casserole dishes and chicken. Was there some newsletter that he did not receive? Was Doreen calling everyone but him with her late-breaking news?

The most perplexing issue to the young pastor was the presence of a retired former pastor in the community. After forty years of pastoring country churches, this sweet country parson had chosen to retire to the small town and joined the church he had once shepherded. He would constantly tell Ergun of his undying loyalty and his willingness to help the young man in any way possible. Their relationship was a blessing to the novice minister with one glaring exception. The retired preacher always beat him to the bedside of a sick member.

The young preacher could not figure this one out! He had deacons who would call him in the event of an accident or a death. He would run to the car, often dressing while driving. His tires would screech to a halt in front of the decedent's home, only to find the retired minister already there. How was this possible?

Approximately one year after arriving at the country church, Ergun discovered the secret weapon in every country gossip's arsenal. This form of gossip, the spreading of information quickly without regard to invasion of privacy or accuracy, was so highly evolved that it confounded the young pastor. Evidently everyone in the community was privy to this fundamental "truth" but him.

Doreen had a *scanner.* So did the old preacher.

While the preacher was studying or watching television, while the deacons were out in the fields or barns, while the members of the church were driving home from their jobs, Doreen would sit in her kitchen, transfixed on that black box that scanned the emergency radio frequencies. Upon hearing of a call to emergency services, Doreen would jump to action, leading a virtual network of gossip lieutenants. Winston Churchill was once quoted as saying that a lie goes around the world before truth has the ability to put on its shoes. Perhaps he was right.

Gossip Is Not Always Malicious; It Is Worse

We must hasten to add that gossip is not always malicious in intent. Indeed, Doreen never seemed to desire to see any harm come to anyone. She was simply curious. In our estimation, this made her infinitely more dangerous.

The Bible seems to make that distinction as well. Peter combines "malice" along with other acts of evil intentions: "So rid yourselves of all wickedness, all deceit, hypocrisy, envy, and all slander" (1 Pet. 2:1). Malice has a desire to see harm come to the victim. It is based on a dark heart.

Gossip is based on curiosity. The millions of *Doreens* who inhabit our churches do not necessarily want to see evil befall another; they just want to know about it when it happens. Biblically, this can be viewed as a chronological issue. Notice the words of the apostle James:

Now when we put bits into the mouths of horses to make them obey us, we also guide the whole animal. And consider ships: though very large and driven by fierce winds, they are guided by a very small rudder wherever the will of the pilot directs. So too, though the tongue is a small part [of the body], it boasts great things. Consider how large a forest a small fire ignites. And the tongue is a fire. The tongue, a world of unrighteousness, is placed among the parts of our [bodies]; it pollutes the whole body, sets the course of life on fire, and is set on fire by hell. (James 3:3–6)

There is a minor, but profound, point to be made. Malicious gossip seeks to see a potential pain to befall the victim. Gossip, according to James, causes pain ("the tongue is a fire") but does not always seek it. It is almost as if James is pleading with the Christians to understand the profundity of their actions. By spreading gossip, the Christian, even without malicious intent, can cause irreparable damage. The malicious, spiteful heart seeks it. The gossip causes it, spreads it, and stokes the flame further simply because they seem to be without hateful intentions.

The malicious heart picks and chooses its intended victim, like a trained marksman. The gossip shoots often and randomly, like an untrained hunter with a shotgun. The "collateral damage" from a gossip is infinitely worse, because he does not know where he is shooting, or how to control it. He shoots because it is in his nature.

A truly infected gossip is not even aware that he is gossiping. In fact, he will be offended when you point out his sin to him. He has been doing it for so long and so often that he knows no other way. It has taken root in his character. It is almost a disease on the genetic level. No one is more illustrative of the gossip gene than Moses' sister, Miriam.

Miriam: The Musician Sister (Exod. 15:19–21)

Miriam enters the pages of biblical history as the first worship leader for the children of God. Celebrating their emancipation from slavery in Egypt, the Israelites marched toward the Red Sea. After the drowning of Pharaoh's army, the children of God celebrated on the far banks of the sea. The Bible illustrates Miriam's leadership in the worship band, leading the instruments, the singing, and the dancing:

> When Pharaoh's horses with his chariots and horsemen went into the sea, the LORD brought the waters of the sea back over them. But the Israelites walked through the sea on dry ground. Then Miriam the prophetess, Aaron's sister, took a tambourine in her hand, and all the women followed her with tambourines and dancing. Miriam sang to them: "Sing to the LORD, for He is highly exalted; He has thrown the horse and its rider into the sea." (Exod. 15:19–21)

Clearly, her leadership was mandated by God, who speaks through Micah and says, "Indeed, I brought you up from the land of Egypt and redeemed you from that place of slavery. I sent Moses, Aaron, and Miriam ahead of you" (Mic. 6:4).

Miriam and the Birth of Gossip (Num. 12:1–15)

Moses' sister and brother did not approve of his new wife, who was from the land of Cush. Rather than come to him directly, they discussed the situation. The symptoms common to the disease of gossip are noticeable from the very start: "Miriam and Aaron criticized Moses because of the Cushite woman he married (for he had married a Cushite woman). They said, 'Does the LORD speak only through Moses? Does He not also speak through us?' And the LORD heard [it]" (Num. 12:1–2).

Moses' choice of a wife angered his siblings. The Septuagint translates this as an "Ethiopian." She was not an Israelite, and obviously, not the woman they wanted in the family. However, rather than bringing their concerns to Moses directly, they began to murmur secretively. The results are always the same: Gossip spreads like a virus.

Traits of Gossip

Gossip always discusses the victim in their absence. They are unable to defend themselves, or even to offer an explanation. However, this does betray another symptom of persons who have a loose tongue: They are cowards. Most gossips would never dream of taking their concerns to the person about whom they are speaking. What fun would that be? Instead, they are satisfied to stand at a distance and discuss in detail the calamities of others.

A second observation about gossip follows in Numbers 12:2: Gossip spreads and builds. At first, the discussion revolved around Moses' marriage. It quickly evolved, however, into a challenge to his leadership. Question Moses' personal wisdom, and soon the discussion is spiraling downward. Gossip is clearly an aggressive form of cancer, spreading quickly.

1. *Gossip is never isolated*. First Moses' wisdom was questioned, and then his leadership was attacked. Even if gossip begins in innocence, it becomes malicious.

2. *Gossip divides*. One can hear Miriam's rationale that she could lead just as easily as Moses. How did she implant that belief in the hearts of the Israelites? By gossip.

3. *Gossip builds up the perpetrator by tearing down the victim*. Miriam questioned Moses' leadership and implicitly placed herself on equal ground with him.

Numbers 12:2 ends with a simple but foreboding statement: "And the LORD heard [it]." We read in the following verse that whatever his response would be, it certainly would be swift, because "*suddenly* the LORD said to Moses." Why would God act with immediacy in this instance?

Because God hates gossip.

Descending on a pillar of cloud, God addressed the siblings directly and without hesitation. "Listen to what I say" (Num. 12:6), he begins. Like a parent to a child that has been caught in a dangerous situation, God takes special care to show that this conversation would go beyond a normal rebuke. This was serious.

God defended Moses as his special and anointed leader. While other leaders in Israel might receive instruction in dreams and visions, God had chosen to speak to Moses unequivocally. Numbers 12:8 continues God's admonition: "I speak with him directly, openly, and not in riddles; he sees the form of the LORD."

The confrontation has an ominous end. God stated, "'So why were you not afraid to speak against My servant Moses?' The LORD's anger *burned against* them, and he left."

Silence enveloped the camp as the threesome stood and watched the cloud lift. Suddenly, Aaron turned and saw that his sister was diseased. Leprosy covered her. Miriam's dead, whitened skin was disintegrating before their eyes. Aaron pleaded with his brother and admitted their sin, and Moses then cried out to the Lord for his sister's healing (Num. 12:10–13). When God replied, he equated her sin with disgrace, and ordered her into a holy "time out." For seven days, Miriam would be separated from the Israelites, and could then return, having been cleansed and made whole again (Num. 12:14–15).

It may sound almost heretical, but we must ask this question, because one can imagine that every gossip, reading these words, is asking the question as well: *Did God overreact?* All Miriam did was just spread a little gossip, share a few "concerns." Did her actions really warrant such a response from God?

As we noted earlier, God hates gossip.

When Gossip Enters the Church: Symptoms and Effects

Two of the Ten Commandments involve slander. The believer is warned not to blaspheme the name of the Lord (Exod. 20:7). To do so is slanderous. Yet the ninth commandment is a warning not to slander another person as well (Exod. 20:16). Why would giving a "false testimony" be equated with the other more heinous sins of murder, adultery, and theft?

When gossip enters the church, it can have far more devastating effects than crimes against the body or possessions. In the eyes of God, gossip is as bad as murder. Examine Leviticus 19:16: "You must not go about spreading slander among your people; you must not jeopardize your neighbor's life." At first glance, it seems like there is a leap in logic here. Were we not just discussing gossip? What does that have to do with jeopardizing a person's life? The marriage of murder and slander is also seen in Exodus 23:7: "Stay far away from a false accusation. Do not kill the innocent and the just, because I will not justify the guilty."

The confusion and fog clears when one reads James's somber words about the effects of gossip: "So too, though the tongue is a small part [of the body], it boasts great things. Consider how large a forest a small fire ignites. And the tongue is a fire. The tongue, a world of unrighteousness, is placed among the parts of our [bodies]; *it pollutes the whole body, sets the course of life on fire, and is set on fire by hell*" (James 3:5–6).

The clear wisdom in James's teaching cannot be ignored: *Murder attacks the body; gossip attacks the soul.*

Solomon's teaching about gossip further illustrates the effects of "just sharing," and give us a window into the diagnosis and effects of the horror of the swollen tongue.

God Hates Gossip in the Church, in All Its Forms

"Six things the LORD hates; in fact, seven are detestable to Him: arrogant eyes, a lying tongue, hands that shed innocent blood, a heart that plots wicked schemes, feet eager to run to evil, a lying witness who gives false testimony, and one who stirs up trouble among brothers" (Prov. 6:16–19).

Traditionally, Christians have focused on the final object of God's hatred—those who "sow seeds of discord" among the brethren. But, a closer look shows that *three* of the seven actions that stir the wrath of God involve the tongue: lying, false testimony, and spreading dissention. In fact, one can see the direct linkage between the tongue and the other wicked acts of plotting false schemes and running swiftly to evil.

We all have tales about people in the local church who seem to revel in fights and confrontations. They get a gleam in their eyes when they start a verbal war between brothers in Christ. They are driven by sin and driven to evil. Proverbs 6:14–15 details their end: He "who plots evil with perversity in his heart— he stirs up trouble constantly. Therefore calamity will strike him suddenly; he will be shattered instantly—beyond recovery."

A Gossip Cannot Keep a Secret

"A gossip goes around revealing a secret, but the trustworthy keeps a confidence" (Prov. 11:13).

The danger of gossips is that they appear to be our trust- worthy friends! No one would ever share a burden of their heart to one they are sure will spread it to others. The gossip comes beside the victim with feigned sympathy and simulates compas- sion. The victim shares some deep pain or problem with the admonition that it not be spread. He might even feel relief after sharing the secret, feeling encouraged that God placed a person in his life to share burdens. The feeling of relief or comfort is quickly replaced with horror when he discovers that the gossip has spread the secret to others. Proverbs 10:18 calls this type of gossip a "fool."

A Gossip Derives His Worth from Your Pain

"A gossip's words are like choice food that goes down to one's innermost being" (Prov. 18:8).

A gossip sees the response in the eyes of the person with whom he shares some salacious story. He feels immediately emboldened. The tragic fact of a habitual gossip is that he devel- ops a sense of superiority at burying others with their words. Their crises, their problems, and their worries seem to diminish in light of the horrible events they are recounting in the life of another. The sense of being on the "inside" makes a gossip feel important, and thus he garners a false sense of "worth."

The lethal component is that, since we are assumed to be in God's house, discussing God's children, the gossip must add an additional dimension to the ruse: he must fake compassion. He will lend his shoulder, and he might even shed a tear. However, the moment the victim is gone, he begins to search his mental files, listing those who would find the news interesting. Even if he had the best intentions to keep the confidence at first, the moment the opportunity arises, he shares your pain.

Gossip Is an Addict's Fix

"Without wood, fire goes out; without a gossip, conflict dies down" (Prov. 26:20).

Once the gossip "breaks" a big story, the rush he feels becomes an addiction. His pulse quickens, and his mind races, attempting to find the next big story. It is more than a disease; it is an addiction. Do you know those Christians who have an abnormal interest in your personal affairs?

See if any of these symptoms resonate: They know the most intimate details about their neighbors. They share invasive prayer requests that make you feel a bit uncomfortable just listening to them. Malignant gossips have a drive and a need to know details. They *thrive* on them.

The worst symptom of a gossip is parallel to the symptoms of a drug addict: He does not see himself as a gossip. In fact, he would be highly offended if you intimated that he is. As the gossip spreads in your community, he is genuinely surprised when you blame him for the problem. The simple fact is, he has an incessant need to stoke the fires of gossip, because when the flame dies down, he needs his "fix."

Gossip Is a Knife in a Friendly Hand

"A hateful person disguises himself with his speech and harbors deceit within. When he speaks graciously, don't believe him" (Prov. 26:24–25).

It would be wise to remember this fundamental principle: No one can hurt your feelings without your permission. That is why gossip is so painful to its victims. It came from a friend. Miriam was Moses' *sister.*

Consider this scenario: A person whom you have never met before approaches you on the street and tells you that your outfit is ugly and your clothes do not match. Do you feel hurt? Do you collapse into anxiety and weep? Of course not. This person's opinion means nothing to you, and if anything, you are bemused that he would even attempt to speak to you.

But if a loved one does the same thing, you would be hurt. Why? Not because his critique was correct, or that he was any wiser than the random stranger, but because he is your friend. The sharpest knives are always in the hands of those whom we thought were our friends.

That is why gossip is so dangerous and antithetical to the church. We are supposed to be a family. We are called to bear one another's burdens to fulfill the law of Christ (Gal. 6:2). If we cannot find empathy, sympathy, and community among fellow believers, is there any hope of finding it among nonbelievers?

Can you see why so many people avoid church? Many times, those who call themselves Christians are worse than nonbelievers because they should know better. They are supposed to be different.

Reluctant Surgeons: Stopping the Outbreak

Few people have to be convinced of the lethal effects of gossip and murmuring. Every day churches split, pastors are fired, and families are irreparably damaged by it. Few diseases are more lethal or more rampant in our churches. One could easily make the case that *glossolitis* among Christians has reached pandemic proportions.

Containing the disease is not easy, but it is essential.

Most pastors and most Christians are in a dilemma. They are aware of the effects of gossip, but they are hesitant to do what must be done to squelch it. Like reluctant surgeons, they stand helplessly over the body, knowing what to do, but unwilling to make the incisions. As in surgery, dealing with gossip is painful, but the alternative is far worse.

One of the most effective means of combating slander is to view it as God sees it—a dangerous threat to hearts and lives, equal to murder. Proverbs 16:28 says, "A contrary man spreads conflict, and a gossip separates friends." Gossip, murmuring, and slander threaten the fellowship we have labored to build. What has taken years to develop can be destroyed in a moment of loose tongues and broken hearts. Without warning, your family and your members will take sides, form allegiances, and counterattack. In a moment's notice, a healthy family and a healthy church become a war zone, complete with hidden land mines. You must act.

Solomon does not seem hesitant in dealing with the slanderer. Proverbs 20:19 ends with the admonition, "Avoid someone with a big mouth."

James also does not waver in the face of the threat of gossip. The third chapter of his book begins with a simple precept that most pastors and leaders would be wise to follow: *Do not put a gossip in any position in the church.* "Not many should become teachers, my brothers, knowing that we will receive a stricter judgment; for we all stumble in many ways. If anyone does not stumble in what he says, he is a mature man who is also able to control his whole body" (James 3:1–2).

A gossip is not mature. A gossip should never be a teacher. A gossip is unbridled. Give a gossip no power and no position, because he will abuse the privilege by sharing secrets entrusted to those in leadership. The entire context of the "tongue" teaching by James in chapter 3 is their influence in the assembly. Give them no influence, and you mute their ability to spread their virus.

James further places the responsibility of stopping the spread of gossip on those who hear it and hear about it. As we noted earlier, the gossip addict is either unaware of his sin or is in deep denial. What can a Christian do to "nip this in the bud"? "My brothers, if any among you strays from the truth, and someone turns him back, he should know that whoever turns a sinner from the error of his way will save his life from death and cover a multitude of sins" (James 5:19–20).

If you do not confront the gossip with his sin in a loving but firm manner, God holds you responsible.

Notice the participants cited by James in the previous text. He says, "if any among *you* strays from the truth." As he was addressing the Christians in general and the leaders specifically, he answers the unspoken question, How do we stop a gossip who is already a teacher, pastor, or leader? You *must* address them and confront the issue, because their responsibility and position means that they will face a *stricter* judgment.

Stop the gossip the moment you sense he is sharing something that does not involve you. Gently say that the information is none of your business. Yes, they will be insulted. Yes, they will become angry at you. Yes, it is even possible that they will begin to gossip about you as a result. But it is worth rescuing them from their sin.

Gossip is a disease that affects the victim, infects the participant, and spreads malignantly through your church like a fire. But it is a preventable disease. The tongue is a "restless evil, full of deadly poison" (James 3:8). Confrontation is the only antidote.

Chapter 4

Myopia: Nearsighted and Shortsighted

Samson and an Achilles Heart
Judges 13–16

Pastor Williams had a knot in his stomach as big as Texas.

Normally, he was a man of great vision and boldness, but that afternoon he was seized with quiet anxiety. He had stood against many enemies of God and had seen God bring great victories against the town's liquor industry and sinful enterprises. But his great secret was now gripping him.

Pastor Williams would rather face a hundred city council meetings than one church business meeting.

In the years he had led the church to which he was called, they had seen great growth. Baptisms, Bible study, and attendance in worship had all been markers of tremendous growth. Now the church was poised to truly change their community. After eighteen months of studies, committees, and preparation, the building and grounds committee, along with the church vision committee, was going to bring the recommendation to the church that they build a new auditorium and educational facility. The vote was scheduled tonight.

The team of twenty people had painstakingly gone through every step of communication possible. They had held "listening sessions," where they received feedback on the various ideas of the members. They had accepted thirty proposals and countless bids on the construction. They had submitted plans to the city and had received approval. They had even mailed out surveys to every church member, faithful in attendance or not, asking for their opinion. They had covered their bases and were satisfied.

Pastor Williams was not. He was terrified.

The surveys had showed that the overwhelming majority of members were in favor of the building and the program. The cost of the project seemed prohibitive, but the people voiced their opinion that this was God's timing and God's plan. Many had even approached the pastor in the ensuing months and offered support of trade, money, and aid. The town was buzzing with the prospect of the first real building project at the church in decades.

Even the non-members in town knew that the church had to do something. Parking was tight. People were walking blocks to the church, since the parking lot often filled up an hour before Bible study even began. The church was packed in all services, and the deacons often had to get folding chairs and place them around the auditorium. The crowds continued to swell, even in the summer vacation months. Something had to be done.

Truly, this night should have been the night of victory. The pastor, many thought, surely was basking in the joy of knowing that finally the church would launch on a great expedition of faith, seizing the moment to change their community and reach their world. Even other pastors jealously prayed, "Lord, give me a people like Pastor Williams has. They have faith. They do what others said was impossible."

But victory was the last thing Pastor Williams had in mind.

All he could think about was Larry Hammett.

Larry Hammett was the most faithful deacon at the church, and easily the longest serving. Through countless pastors, Larry had grown up in the church. His mother and father had raised him there. It was the church in which he was saved, baptized, and married. He had seen his children grow up there and was now enjoying seeing his grandchildren attend. Every Sunday, Larry was the first to arrive, the first to serve, and the last to leave. Larry was a faithful servant of Christ, and he was not going to let this vote go through without a fight.

Larry Hammett never met a proposal, vote, or program that he did not dislike. He was seemingly genetically incapable of voting yes on anything. It mattered little what the motion was: new chairs, changed service times, the purchase of a bus, etc. In every instance, Larry not only voted against the measure; he also led the charge against it.

As Pastor Williams suspected, the upcoming vote was no different.

Having faced such measures before, Larry knew what had to be done. Quietly, almost imperceptibly, Larry had begun his work when the committee was formed. Through eighteen months, he watched with suspicion as ideas were bandied about. Proposals of millions of dollars were thrown around as if they were advertisements. Finally the committees had printed their proposal and presented it to the church after a Sunday morning service. In two weeks, he heard, the church was going to vote on the proposal in business meeting on a Wednesday night. As Larry calculated in his head, he had seventeen days to get his "ducks in a row."

He knew exactly what to do.

Larry knew that if he appeared too adamantly against the measure, he would be perceived as a "troublemaker." He could not risk that. If he seemed to make the issue a personal vendetta against the pastor, people would discount him as a man with an agenda. Even though no one in the church could remember a time when Larry had actually voted for doing anything new, he had to appear to be a reasonable and loving deacon—a Christian who felt the conviction that this was not a good idea. He had to be very careful.

First, he planted a measure of doubt in the minds of his Bible study class members. For decades, he had taught the same forty or fifty people, and they were the core of the church leadership. Even though a few of them served on the two committees that were bringing the recommendation, Larry felt he could sway them as well. He had done it before. He used his Bible study lesson to teach that stewardship was a judicious protection of God's provision. "Rushing into anything that would unwisely use the precious resources that God gave us," he taught, "was an abuse of his loving provision."

Secondly, he worked hard to appear to be a reasonable man. He loved the pastor deeply, he would tell members, but he had questions about such a project that would risk losing everything for which he and the pastor had worked so hard. He was just thinking about the great testimony of the church, he reasoned. If this fails, he proposed, it would ruin the reputation of the church!

Finally, he began to speak to the elderly men and women of the church, many of whom were the biggest givers and his closest friends. He spoke of the loss of legacy. The loss of that Sunday school class where they had been taught as children. Did they remember that? He would point to an abandoned small room, now used for storage of folding chairs, and say, "Hey, wasn't this Preacher Thompson's old office? Wow, it will be a shame to lose this room. Hey Selma," he said to one elderly woman, "weren't you saved in that office back in 1943?" Of course, he knew she was. He was counting on it.

In the ensuing seventeen days after the announcement, Larry became a one-man phone machine. In fact, he called every elderly member, friend, and leader he knew. Drawing from his copy of the membership roster, he also played his trump card: He called every inactive member on the roster. Many of them had long since stopped attending the church for various reasons.

Many of them did not even know the name of the present pastor, who had been there only eleven years. They were now—the vast majority of them—not only inactive members but also nonpracticing Christians. They had not attended in years, not even for funerals. Others were attending other churches or had moved to a neighboring city.

But this did not matter to Larry Hammett. The only thing that mattered to him was that each one he called had never transferred his membership to another church. He made the same speech every time: He would ask them about their children and grandchildren, and then after the pleasantries, he would get to the point: This new pastor was threatening the church of their youth. With his newfangled ideas and young leaders, he was going to destroy that old church that had meant so much to them all. Could they come and support him—one lowly deacon—one last time? Even though they had not attended a single service since Pastor Williams had arrived, they were still members. They still had the right to vote. On the appointed Wednesday, he needed them to do so.

At precisely 6:45 PM on Wednesday evening, Pastor Williams drove up to the church to find the parking lot filled with cars he did not recognize. As he walked into the auditorium, he saw faces he did not recognize. The church was so full that people were sitting on the steps leading to the balcony. People mingled, catching up on fifteen years of absence. Immediately, Pastor Williams knew what was happening. In the corner of his eye, he saw Larry Hammett. Focusing his attention on Larry— this deacon who had served for so long—he *knew*. Larry would not even make eye contact with the pastor. The fix was in. The vote was squashed.

What would cause someone like Deacon Larry Hammett to labor so diligently against each and every vote for progress in the church? He was afflicted.

He was afflicted with the disease of spiritual myopia.

It is epidemic in our time.

Spiritual Myopia: The Symptoms of Samson

Spiritual myopia is a disease so rampant in Christianity today that it has affected every single church. More than likely, you were picturing a carrier of spiritual myopia while you were reading this fictitious tale. You were inserting the names of your own "Larry" as you read, weren't you?

Spiritually myopic Christians are often people who are the most faithful before the Lord. They can be pastors, deacons, teachers, ushers, or laymen. They have often invested their lives and resources in the Lord's work, and yet they can spread their contagion so quickly that they irreparably damage God's churches. They have a living illustration of their disease in the life of the great Old Testament warrior, Samson.

Samson was born of a miracle. In Judges 13, we are told of a couple who was unable to have children. The husband, Manoah, and his wife lamented that God had not blessed them with a child. Then Judges 13:3–5 tells us:

> The Angel of the LORD appeared to the woman and
> said to her, "It is true that you are barren and have no
> children, but you will conceive and give birth to a son.
> Now please be careful not to drink wine or other alco-
> holic beverages, or to eat anything unclean; for indeed,
> you will conceive and give birth to a son. You must
> never cut his hair, because the boy will be a Nazirite to
> God from birth, and he will begin to save Israel from
> the power of the Philistines."

She quickly ran and told her husband. Manoah, who was a faithful Israelite from the tribe of Dan, prayed that the angel would appear again, and tell him exactly how to raise the son. Neither he nor his wife realized at the time that they were experiencing a theophany—an appearance of God himself—but they would in a moment.

Judges 13:9–14 tells us that the Lord appeared to Manoah and his wife again, while the wife was working in the fields. Amazed at the miraculous promise of God, Manoah offered to fix the "angel" a meal of goat meat. The Lord deferred his hospitality but instead told Manoah to prepare a burnt offering to the Lord. When Manoah prepared the goat and placed it on a rock along with a grain offering as well, the Lord lighted it with fire.

At that moment, Manoah and his wife saw another miracle — the angel of the Lord ascending in the flame! The couple immediately understood that they had just seen God, and they threw themselves on the ground in worship. In Judges 13:22, Manoah even exclaimed, "We're going to die . . . because we have seen God!" If the birth of their son would be proclaimed by God himself, they reasoned, surely he was to be a miraculous and mighty man. They named their son Samson.

Samson: Squandered Blessings (Judg. 14–15)

The exploits of this mighty man called by God are legendary. Yet what remains of his legacy is the nagging recognition that he was a man who never considered his future in his actions. Impetuous to a fault, Samson is a living reminder of those who can never see beyond their own narrow vision. In his nearsightedness, Samson illustrates a life of squandered opportunities.

Judges 14 narrates Samson's pursuit of a wife. On his way to the Philistine town of Tamnah to get a wife, he tore a lion apart with his bare hands (Judg. 14:3–7). Was this a mark of rage or impetuousness? No, because the Bible clearly states that the "Spirit of the LORD took control of him" (Judg. 14:6). However, as is often the case in the life of Samson, he could be in the midst of a holy moment, seeing God work directly through him, and snatch defeat from the jaws of victory!

When Samson was returning to claim his wife, he came upon the carcass of the lion he had killed. He reached into the carcass of the lion, put his hand into a nest of bees, and pulled out the honey to eat (Judg. 14:8–9). At the wedding feast, Samson used the honey as a riddle that he told to the men of his bride's village. At this juncture we begin to see Samson's fatal flaw—his nearsightedness.

When the riddle perplexed the Philistine men, they cajoled his bride to manipulate the answer from Samson. After crying

and nagging for seven days, the woman finally convinced
Samson to tell her the secret. A week later the marriage ended
horrifically.

Many Bible scholars believe that Samson illustrates a life of
impetuous lust, driven to pursue his deepest longings and fleshly
desires. These traits are present in Samson, to be sure. But we
believe these traits are symptoms of a disease far more dangerous.
The symptoms betray an underlying problem. Samson's greatest
weakness was not lust, rage, or violence. These faults were symptomatic of his struggle to get beyond the immediate present.
Remember, what a mighty lion could not do, a woman's tears
accomplished. Samson's weakness was not his strength but his
vision.

His immediate desires were always Samson's biggest concern. In his twenty years as a judge of Israel (Judg. 15:20),
Samson's most devastating trait was his inability to see the future
blessings as a product of present obedience. Future consequences meant little to Samson. Whatever he needed right now
was his obsession. Thirsty? Give me drink now! Lust? Find me
a woman! He was willing to gamble the future that God had
promised him for his present satisfaction and security.

It must be clearly stated that this is not the story of an evil
unbeliever who squanders God's salvation for any diversion.
Four times in the narrative the Bible tells us that the "Spirit of the
LORD" took control of Samson (Judg. 13:25; 14:6; 14:19; 15:14).
No, this is the tale of a man with the power of God upon him, but
who tragically abandoned his future. His weeping wife from
Tamnah was a harbinger of horrible destruction for Samson.
This seems to be the pattern in a spiritually myopic person; they
never learn the lessons of the past.

Samson's Perpetual Flaw: Spiritual Astigmatism (Judg. 16:4–20)

Perhaps the most famous and most tragic part of Samson's
story is his disastrous affair with Delilah. It probably started

with him seeing her, just as we are told in Judges 14:1: "Samson went down to Timnah and saw a young Philistine woman." It is amazing how he was able to focus his sight on all the wrong things but could not see what God wanted him to do when it was right in front of his face. He probably just spotted her walking down the street, and his out-of-control desires took control of him once again.

When the Philistine nobles discovered Samson's preoccupation with this young woman, they offered her enormous amounts of money and so purchased for themselves the possibility of defeating this famous foe.

Her first three attempts to discover the secret of Samson's strength failed miserably. She would ask Samson what was the secret of his strength, and he would give her some ridiculous answer. She would pass that along to her handlers, and they would provide her with what she needed. This reminds us of Lex Luther, who was constantly trying to find the flaw in Superman.

You begin to wonder after the first time Delilah tried to bind him why Samson did not catch on. Why did he not see it coming? Perhaps because his myopia had degenerated into an *astigmatism*, the inability to focus on anything. Everything was out of balance, out of focus, and he could not see anything well.

The scene that follows is unbelievable. The Bible student reads this and wonders how this could happen. Samson has his head in Delilah's lap, she calls the Philistine lords in and tells them to shave off his hair (Judg. 16:19). One of the most tragic statements in all of Scripture sums up the result of Samson's myopia: "He did not know that the LORD had left him" (Judg. 16:20). Samson was seized by the Philistines, who had waited for this moment for years. We are told that they seized him and gouged out his eyes. The truth is that he had been spiritually blind for some time.

It began with a simple incident that ended with this tragic scene. Do you recall when Samson killed the lion, a great display of God's power in his life? On a return trip back home, he went looking for the carcass of that animal. He found it and discovered that bees had built a nest in it, and there was honey. He reached down into that dead carcass and scooped up a handful of honey, and we are told that he took it to his father and mother.

When he gave them the honey, there is an interesting statement made: "He did not tell them that he had scooped the honey from the lion's carcass" (Judg. 14:9).

Now why would Scripture make this point? It is because Samson knew that if he told his parents that he had touched something dead, they would be horrified. Part of his Nazarite vow kept him from touching anything dead. His spiritual myopia began then. It progressively became worse. *Presbyopia* is a condition where the eyesight deteriorates. It is caused by aging. *Spiritual presbyopia* is caused by an unrepentant spirit that continues to walk deeper and deeper into spiritual darkness. It is a refusal to allow any spiritual light to shine on our decisions and choices.

Samson's Fatal Flaw: Spiritual Presbyopia (Judg. 16:21–27)

The end of Samson's life is as tragic as the beginning was heroic. The narrative continues in Judges 16:21–27:

The Philistines seized him and gouged out his eyes. They brought him down to Gaza and bound him with bronze shackles, and he was forced to grind grain in the prison. But his hair began to grow back after it had been shaved. Now the Philistine leaders gathered together to offer a great sacrifice to their god Dagon. They rejoiced and said:

Our god has handed over
our enemy Samson to us.

When the people saw him, they praised their god and said:

Our god has handed over to us
our enemy who destroyed our land
and who multiplied our dead.

When they were drunk, they said, "Bring Samson here
to entertain us." So they brought Samson from prison,
and he entertained them. They had him stand between
the pillars.

Samson said to the young man who was leading him
by the hand, "Lead me where I can feel the pillars supporting the temple, so I can lean against them." The
temple was full of men and women; all the leaders of the
Philistines were there, and about 3,000 men and women
were on the roof watching Samson entertain [them].

Can you imagine the scene? Can you imagine the irony?
Here was Samson, the once-mighty judge of Israel, now performing like a circus monkey before those who mocked God!
This must have been a surreal scene for the thousands in attendance. It is even more tragic for those of us who know his story
from the biblical record.

Samson had killed thousands of Philistines with just the jaw-
bone of a donkey. He defended the honor of the name of the Lord
during his life. If you were a spectator at the event, would you
not have shouted to Samson to do something? Knowing Samson
through the Bible, we imagine that if we were spectators to the
tragedy, we would have stood in disbelief. We would have
assumed that Samson was only entertaining them to trick them.
Surely he had a plan?

Yet Samson just entertained the crowd. The once-mighty
warrior was now just a clown. Could he not see that?

The incongruity of referencing the inability to see by a blind
man is not lost on us. It serves as an illustration of the final ravages of the disease of spiritual myopia: The victim is the last to
recognize the disease. Like the proverbial frog in the kettle, the
loss of vision is so incremental and so subtle that the person suffering from the disease rarely recognizes his limitations. He learns
to adjust, almost unconsciously, and moves on. In Samson's case,
he was unaware of how ridiculous and tragic he looked. He was
simply resigned to his fate. He felt he had no other choice.

If impetuousness is one dimension of spiritual myopia, then stagnation and spiritual inertia represent the other extreme. Some Christians have become so myopic that they cannot see that the disease has left them unwilling to move anywhere. As Samson begged the man who led him into the temple, these Christians cannot move without hesitation and without help.

Let us make it even more emphatic.

Have you ever met a Christian who simply could not envision God's great plan for his life? Through the years, he had developed a cynicism, and no matter how much you told him that God could do a mighty work through him, he stubbornly refused to believe it. This is the last stage of spiritual myopia.

Have you ever seen a church, standing on the precipice of greatness, choose instead to do nothing, and get passed by and become insignificant and ineffective? This is the result of spiritual myopia.

Two generations ago, a church in a major city had a visionary pastor. His preaching was invigorating, and he challenged the people to claim their mountain for God. The church was situated just on the outskirts of the central nexus of the city, and plans were in motion to expand the city toward them. Within years, the pastor told the people, they would be right in the heart of the city. It was time to act.

Around the pastor's tenth anniversary, a member of the church approached the pastor. He owned the ten acres next to the church, and wanted to donate the land. This man, a casual member of the church to that point, believed the pastor's vision. If they wanted to claim their land and reach the city, he wanted to help.

The pastor was ecstatic. Finally, he thought, the church was going to be able to do what the Lord had given them the vision to do. Immediately he began to pray about the use of the land. Their facilities could barely hold those who were already attending. They could use the land to build a new sanctuary. Their nursery and children's facilities were already inadequate. They could add a new area that would be inviting to young couples with children. The parking lot was woefully small. People were already parking on the lawn beside the church. They could add parking. His head was spinning with ideas, and the fact that the land was being offered at no cost was beyond his wildest dreams. He spent the days leading to the Sunday service praising God.

The Sunday evening service was a letdown.

At the specially called business meeting, the pastor shared the wonderful news about the donation of land. With tears in his eyes, he told the church of the amazing potential of the acreage and the value of such a gracious gift. Truly, he concluded, this donation would enable the church to reach the city and lead many people to Christ. For the pastor, and for some of the members, this was a visitation and blessing from God.

Slowly, however, older members of the church rose to speak. They offered objections that shocked the pastor. They spoke of costs, plans, limitations, and processes. They spoke of city planners, diagrams, building codes, easements, blueprints, and the costs involved in every phase. He was dumbfounded.

Other members rose to say that they liked the church the way it was. They were not sure they wanted so many new people to attend. They did not want new wings added or a new sanctuary built. Sure, a new sanctuary could seat more people, but the old one had been built by their grandparents, and they hated to see it go. In an all-too-familiar method, the membership shot down the plan. With a resounding voice, they rejected the offer of the free land.

These church members were suffering from advanced myopia. They were suffering the effects of presbyopia, the degenerative form of myopia that gradually and progressively leaves the person (and the church) blind. Regardless of the explanation, and regardless of the potential, all they could see was the immediate steps in front of them. The "big picture" meant nothing to them. Like Samson, they did not realize how ridiculous and wretched they had become.

Decades have passed since that day. True to expectation, the city did expand in their direction, and today, millions of people pass that ten-acre region that was once offered to the church. The benefactor who offered the church the land eventually sold it for millions of dollars and retired. As a silent, anonymous spectator of that business meeting, he left the church that night. Shortly thereafter, the pastor also left, dejected and heartbroken.

And the church? As the city expanded toward them and developments grew all around them, they maintained their stubborn stance as a small church on the thoroughfare. A few years later, with the membership having dwindled and died off, the remaining few members sold the building, gave the money to the local association, and disbanded. The site is now part of a strip mall. All that remains is the sad memories of what could have been.

The church had died of myopia. The older leadership within the church did not have a vision for the future. All they could see was their love for the past and their fears in the present. Myopia can be fatal.

In Mac's first church was a deacon who never came to a single Wednesday night Bible study unless there was a business meeting. Then he came—and no matter what the issue, what the need, what the ministry opportunity, he had two questions that he always asked in an attempt to derail whatever the church was about to do. The questions were: "How much will it cost, and who is going to pay for it?" He could have been called "Old Faithful," because he was going to spew every month at business meeting time.

On one occasion when this deacon came to Mac's office, he gave some insight into why he always was at business meetings and why he was so myopic in his views. He informed the pastor that he had a copy of every business report in that church for the past thirty years. He could go back with precision and rehearse every figure, what was said, and the vote, because he kept copious notes and filed them. To him *that* was church!

He was so myopic that he could only see dollar signs. Everything about the church, the kingdom of God, and God's people was relegated to a dollar amount. That had taken place for so long that no spiritual light could break through.

Do you know anyone with myopia? Can you recognize the symptoms? Do you know a person, a leader, or a church who

- fails to see the big picture because small obstacles obscure the view,
- knows the cost of everything but the value of nothing,
- is perpetually cynical, but sees themselves as "practical," and
- never sees beyond the cost and never realizes the investment?

If you do, then you understand. And if this describes you, then you might end up like Samson. Having lost all dignity and hope, Samson clung to one final option. Knowing that he was no longer capable to lead, he fell on his proverbial sword. In Judges 16:28–30, Samson's final prayer and action are recorded:

He called out to the LORD: "Lord GOD, please remember me. Strengthen me, God, just once more. With one act of vengeance, let me pay back the Philistines for my two eyes." Samson took hold of the two middle pillars supporting the temple and leaned against them, one on his right hand and the other on his left. Samson said, "Let me die with the Philistines." He pushed with all his might, and the temple fell on the leaders and all the people in it. And the dead he killed at his death were more than those he had killed in his life.

Though we often preach and teach otherwise, this was not an act of heroism; it was an act of desperation. Having seen the horrific results of a lifetime of bad choices and limited vision, Samson took himself out of the game. Notice that he did not even ask the Lord to defend the honor of his name or that of his children. Samson was selfish to the end. He asked for retribution on those who had taken his eyes. No spiritual reason. No honorable defense of the Lord who had called him. Samson was blind, suffering from advancing myopia to the end.

It was a Sunday afternoon when the sun began to set at the 2003 Doral Championship in Miami, Florida. Everybody was standing and waiting on Scott Hoch to make his nine-foot birdie putt on the second playoff hole.

But Hoch was unsure about the lay of the green. He put on hold the tournament's sudden-death finish until the next morning. The fans did not like it, but that was Hoch's decision.

The next morning when play resumed, Hoch sank that nine-foot birdie putt and then birdied the third hole to win $900,000 and the Doral. If Hoch had attempted that putt the evening before when the light was poor, he probably would have lost. In the dwindling light Hoch, who has had five eye operations, thought the putt would break and move to the left. His caddie saw it the other way. The next morning in the bright Florida morning light, it turned out that the caddie was right [Associated Press article by Doug Fersuson (3–11–03).

Making decisions in the light—God's light—is the answer to the myopia that plagues the church in these days of spiritual darkness.

Chapter 5

Arteriosclerosis: Harden Not Your Heart

Nabal and the Heart of Stone
1 Samuel 25:1–39

On the day Bobbie Dean died, he went into eternity with all the stubbornness with which he had lived. Growling at his nurses in the hospital, he even dismissed his visitors with a wave. He told them to stop hovering like vultures, and even promised that he would outlive them all.

On that quiet Saturday afternoon, Bobbie Dean was greeted in heaven by the Lord, and if he was consistent, he probably complained about his surroundings then as well.

He had outlived his wife by fifteen years, though some in their small community conjectured that she had died simply to get away from him. He was, to say the least, a grouch. Few had ever seen him smile, and even fewer people remembered a time when he was happy or satisfied. He worked hard and expected everyone around him to do so as well. He was at work on his farm before sunrise and got off the tractor after sunset.

And yet as odd as it may sound, he never missed a Sunday morning service at the church. Precisely at the beginning of the worship hour, he would enter the church, survey the bulletin, and then cross his arms and listen to the sermon. He fancied himself a critic of preaching, and this latest preacher was clearly his favorite. Still, this did not mean that the pastor could escape his often contemptuous gaze.

"Quit calling for people to make decisions," Bobbie would propose. "It never does any good."

At first the minister thought the advice came from his dislike of the community. But it turned out that Bobbie's position had a far deeper implication. One day after a service (and another long invitation) the preacher mustered up the courage to ask the old codger why he always disparaged giving people the opportunity to make public decisions.

"Well, there ain't no reason," he said with a firm stare. "I came forward sixty years ago, and got saved and baptized, and I have never seen the reason to come forward since."

The gentleman's words shocked the preacher.

"You mean you have not come forward in sixty years? Not even to pray for someone else, or rededicate your life, or even settle an issue with which you have been struggling?" the preacher asked.

"No I haven't," the man said definitively. "Rededication is just a bunch of 'preacher talk.' There ain't no need to do it. We all struggle, but I have never fallen into any sin so deep as to merit such a 'decision.' Besides, whenever I felt bad back then, I just waited a while, and the feeling went away. Nowadays, I don't even feel that anymore. Preacher, that's called maturity!"

No. That is called spiritual arteriosclerosis. Though the elderly farmer died from a variety of ailments, he was also afflicted with a spiritual condition known as a hardened heart. He had long since abandoned being sensitive to the call of God, the voice of God, and the work of God. He was spiritually hardened, yet saved. He was stiff-necked, bull-headed, and miserable.

Sadly, those who are afflicted with this spiritual ailment make everyone around them miserable as well.

Spiritual Arteriosclerosis Examined: Calluses of the Heart

In the medical field, arteriosclerosis is a condition from the hardening of the arteries. Plaque and other impurities develop in the blood vessels, and it becomes difficult for blood to flow through them. Eventually, entire arteries can become blocked, and death becomes imminent unless emergency surgery is performed. Sometimes it takes years for this condition to develop. Such factors as a poor diet and a lack of exercise contribute to it.

In the spiritual arena, the onslaught of such a disease is equally as slow. The plaque, in this case, is a deliberate hardening of one's heart toward the Word of God and the voice of God. The Christian who had been sensitive to the voice of God at conviction and conversion now deliberately ignores the admonitions of God in his life. He willfully sins, or he ignores God's call to service, submission, or repentance. Eventually, without true penitence, he will become as hardened as many of the non-Christians who watch his sinful ways. Though he is saved, and was truly converted in previous days, he is now an embarrassment to the church of God.

Picture the process this way: Imagine you scratch your forearm because it itches. You scratch and you scratch, and eventually the itch goes away. However, in your vigor to scratch your forearm, you have inflamed the area, and now it is injured worse than when you first felt the itch! Contrary to medical advice, you continue to scratch it.

Inevitably, your body reacts to the injury. The body produces a callous or a scab in order to protect that injured area. This defense mechanism of your body was created by God to protect the injured area. However, the callous continues to grow in direct proportion to the rigors of the scratching. Eventually, a strong callous develops on your forearm.

Does your forearm hurt when you scratch it now? Not as much. The callous prevents you from feeling the scratch. Does this make sense? Eventually, you can scratch just as hard as you did the first time you scratched it, but you barely feel the grating. You have grown desensitized to the scratching, even though you may be scratching just as vigorously.

Nabal and the Heart of Stone (1 Sam. 25:1–39)

Few biblical characters are as illustrative of this condition as the man known as Nabal. He was the perfect picture of someone who had experienced every blessing of the protection of God and was miserable as a consequence. As we examine the narrative, you will begin to see characteristics of others you may know who, though blessed of God, demonstrate the arrogance of ignorance.

Nabal was a wealthy rancher and a Calebite who lived under the protection of King David. His wealth had allowed him to do business in his hometown of Maon as well as neighboring cities. The Bible tells us that he had three thousand sheep and one thousand goats and had traveled to Carmel to do the shearing of the wool.

Our first inclination of Nabal's character is the description he receives in 1 Samuel 25:3. He "was harsh and evil in [his] dealings." Yet as his wife, Abigail, notes later in the chapter, his name is also an indicator of his character. *Nabal* means "fool" (1 Sam. 25:25).

David was returning from the burial service for the prophet Samuel, and he and his men were hungry. Hearing that Nabal was nearby, David sent ten young men to visit Nabal. David's instructions were clear: Bring greetings and peace to Nabal and his family and then ask him for some food so that we may eat. Remind him that we have protected him and his sheep, and he has experienced the favor of God (1 Sam. 25:4–8).

David's guards did as they were instructed. But instead of being greeted by a grateful subject in David's kingdom, Nabal lashed out in arrogance. "Nabal asked them, 'Who is David? Who is Jesse's son? Many slaves these days are running away from their masters. Am I supposed to take my bread, my water, and my meat that I butchered for my shearers and give them to men who are from I don't know where?'" (1 Sam. 25:10–11).

Do not mistake Nabal's sarcasm for an actual question. He knew exactly who King David was, and he indicated as much when he cited David's father. Neither was this an issue of Nabal not having enough to feed both his own workers and David's. His concern was the loss of money, as seen in his statement that it was for his "shearers." Nabal had come to Carmel to do business. King David's request was going to cost him money.

Immediately upon receiving the report of Nabal's words, David gathered four hundred men and led them to confront Nabal. One of Nabal's workers, certainly a recipient of Nabal's wrath and anger previously, understood the gravity of the situation. He found Nabal's wife, Abigail, and reported the danger to her:

Look, David sent messengers from the wilderness to greet our master, but he yelled at them. The men treated us well. When we were in the field, we weren't harassed and nothing of ours was missing the whole time we were living among them. They were a wall around us, both day and night, the entire time we were herding the sheep. Now consider carefully what you must do, because there is certain to be trouble for our master and his entire family. He is such a worthless fool nobody can talk to him! (1 Sam. 25:14–17)

To prevent a war based solely on her husband's insolence, Abigail prepared a meal herself and carried it down the mountain pass to meet David and his warriors. She had prepared two hundred loaves of bread, five butchered sheep, two hundred fig cakes, roasted grain, and some wine (1 Sam. 25:18–20).

When she encountered King David and his army, Abigail prostrated herself on the ground before him, begging for his mercy. Even though the crime had been committed by her husband, Abigail wasted no time in bearing the full brunt of the responsibility herself. Notice her words of humility:

When Abigail saw David, she quickly got off the donkey and fell with her face to the ground in front of David. She fell at his feet and said, "The guilt is mine, my lord, but please let your servant speak to you directly. Listen to the words of your servant. My lord should pay no attention to this worthless man Nabal, for he lives up to his name. His name is Nabal, and stupidity is all he knows. I, your servant, didn't see my lord's young men whom you sent. Now my lord, as surely as the LORD lives and as you yourself live, it is the LORD who kept you from participating in bloodshed and avenging yourself by your own hand. May your enemies and those who want trouble for my lord be like Nabal. Accept this gift your servant has brought to my lord, and let it be given to the young men who follow my lord. Please forgive your servant's offense, for the LORD is certain to make a lasting dynasty for my lord because he fights the LORD's battles. Throughout your life, may evil not be found in you." (1 Sam. 25:23–28)

Abigail also showed why she was a faithful servant of God. Not only was she knowledgeable of the work and words of God, but was also capable of repentance and humility, both of which Nabal lacked. She praised David, but she mainly praised the God that King David served. She continued:

"When someone pursues you and attempts to take your life, my lord's life will be tucked safely in the place where the LORD your God protects the living. However, He will fling away your enemies' lives like (stones) from a sling. When the LORD does for my lord all the good He promised and appoints you ruler over

Israel, there will not be remorse or a troubled conscience for my lord because of needless bloodshed or
my lord's revenge. And when the LORD does good
things for my lord, may you remember [me] your
servant." (1 Sam. 25:29–31)

David's response to Abigail is similar to God's response to a
repentant Israel: He not only forgives her, but he also blesses her.
The difference between the responses of Nabal and Abigail are
significant for those who struggle with the hardening of their
heart. Abigail was a "discerning" and "blessed" woman who was
both humble and giving. Nabal, who also lived under David's
protection, was "arrogant" and "vile." Listen to David's words to
this poor wife of an unrepentant Nabal:

Then David said to Abigail, "Praise to the LORD God of
Israel, who sent you to meet me today! Blessed is your
discernment, and blessed are you. Today you kept me
from participating in bloodshed and avenging myself by
my own hand. Otherwise, as surely as the LORD God of
Israel lives, who prevented me from harming you, if
you had not come quickly to meet me, Nabal wouldn't
have had any men left by morning light." Then David
accepted what she had brought him and said, "Go home
in peace. See, I have heard what you said and have
granted your request." (1 Sam. 25:32–35)

Tragedy averted. Based entirely on Abigail's meekness,
Nabal's entire workforce and family were saved. One would
think that forestalling a massacre would have given Nabal a
cause to contemplate his decisions. Imagine, an entire battle
based upon your anger, sarcasm, and lack of concern. Would you
not reconsider your behavior?

Not Nabal.

He was unaware that his wife had saved his life and the lives
of his people. All he knew was that David's men had left in a
hurry, and his own servants were terrified that his rage was going
to cause a bloodbath. Perhaps his party was his response to his
imminent death, or just his standard method of operation:

Whenever trouble rises, act as if nothing is wrong. Perhaps Nabal was so calloused that nothing concerned him at this point. One of the clear signs of a frozen conscience is the absence of concern. Nabal simply did not care.

What do we find Nabal doing on the eve of his looming death? "Then Abigail went to Nabal, and there he was in his house, feasting like a king. Nabal was in a good mood and very drunk, so she didn't say anything to him until morning light" (1 Sam. 25:36).

The Lord offers us a little "word play" here. The phrase "in a good mood" is literally translated, "his heart was good on him," or "his heart was good *in* him." In a fictional novel, this would be called a harbinger. His heart failure the next morning is in stark contrast to the "happy" heart he had when he was drunk.

The next morning, Nabal was sober, and Abigail told him how he had averted death. The Bible clearly describes his demise: "In the morning when Nabal sobered up, his wife told him about these events. Then he had a seizure and became paralyzed. About 10 days later, the LORD struck Nabal dead" (1 Sam. 25:37–38). Focus on the two terms *seizure* and *paralyzed*. The word *seizure* can be translated in the Hebrew as, "his heart died within him." The term *paralyzed* is even more descriptive. In the Hebrew, it means, "his heart became like a stone."

Ten days later, Nabal died, but the irony of this tale is this: Nabal was dead long before breath left his body. He was dead the moment he became calloused to the word of God. His stone heart had developed over a long period of time, through his lessening sensitivity to God and his provision. He was a dead man walking.

Implications of Spiritual Arteriosclerosis

We are on dangerous ground here. This is not a subject to be taken lightly. To what extent does a believer's hardening heart go? Is there a consequence to the believer who refuses to repent for sins committed after salvation?

Consider Nabal's sin as an isolated incident. Would it not seem somewhat capricious for God to strike Nabal dead for simply insulting King David and refusing to give hospitality? If those sins were the standard for God's judgment, how many others would be in his divine crosshairs?

This is a much deeper ailment than an act of impious language and selfishness. Like the physical equivalent of arteriosclerosis, the spiritual component takes time to develop. Nabal's death was not in relation to an isolated incident, but rather the culmination of years of disobedience. It was a *result*, not the cause.

Christians are aware of the consequences of a lost person's stubbornness to the voice of God in conviction. In a notorious case, God promised Moses he would harden Pharaoh's heart, so that the miraculous release of the Israelites could take place and the defeat of the Egyptians would be complete. Among the citations is Exodus 4:21: "The LORD instructed Moses, 'When you go back to Egypt, make sure you do in front of Pharaoh all the wonders I have put within your power. But I will harden his heart so that he won't let the people go'" (see also Exod. 7:3; 14:4, 17).

Does this indicate that the hardening of a nonbeliever's heart is within God's will? Does this mean that God desires people to go to hell?

We must hasten to answer that numerous citations prove that God does not desire anyone to go to hell. If the Lord would have hardened Pharaoh's heart just once, and it remained hard, then perhaps those who propose this view might have a point. But God hardened Pharaoh's heart a number of times.

Why? Why would he have to harden Pharaoh's heart more than once?

If God would have hardened Pharaoh's heart permanently, would not the subsequent "hardenings" be redundant? Was hardening a "heart of stone" even harder?

Or could it be that the Pharaoh's heart softened and returned to normalcy after the confrontation? In that case, then the hardening was for a specific time and purpose. Following the confrontation, Pharaoh was returned to a heart that was capable of repentance. Add to that the fact that Pharaoh hardened his heart himself (Exod. 8:15, 32; 9:34), and one sees that he was responsible for his actions.

The Warning to the Jewish Nation (Heb. 3:1–15)

The next pertinent citation is the dual warnings against "hardening" one's heart. In most cases, pastors and preachers make the citation in relation to the infidel hardening their heart toward the conviction by the Holy Spirit to salvation. The faithful Jewish audience is admonished twice, "Today, if you hear His voice, do not harden your hearts as in the rebellion," (Heb. 3:7–8, 15). This warning is repeated in Hebrews 4:7.

The counsel would not have been lost on a faithful and mature Israelite. He would remember exactly the same words of the Psalmist in Psalm 95:7–8. He would also remember the promise of God given twice in the writings of Ezekiel:

And I will give them one heart and put a new spirit
within them; I will remove their heart of stone from their
bodies and give them a heart of flesh. (Ezek. 11:19)

I will give you a new heart and put a new spirit
within you; I will remove your heart of stone and give
you a heart of flesh. (Ezek. 36:26)

The choice, for the Israelites, for Nabal, and for all of us is to choose a heart of flesh that is sensitive to the work and voice of God, or you will develop a heart of stone, impermeable to his conviction. You will end up like Nabal.

One of the saddest experiences of Mac's ministry took place recently. A woman in his church had a lost husband, who had begun attending the services. Mac was sure that the man was getting closer and closer to salvation every week. However, the woman became obsessed with her anger toward President George W. Bush. As Pastor Mac had been invited to meet with the president in the White House, this woman took that to mean that he was going to begin preaching on politics. Though Mac never did preach on politics, the woman began incessantly calling the church office every week, yelling about the political issues of the day.

In the meantime, Pastor Mac was developing a relationship with the husband. He was sure he was nearing the time when he would accept Christ as Savior.

The opportunity never came.

The woman, blinded by her rage, stopped coming to church. Her heart was so hardened that she was willing to gamble on her husband's eternal destiny in order to satisfy some political affiliation. This is the very definition of a hardened heart.

The Warning to Perpetually Rebellious Christians (1 John)

Can a believer harden his heart to the voice of the God that saved him? Can a Christian, once saved, become rebellious, and once in that rebellion, choose not to listen to the Father? What would the implications of such a condition be?

The apostle John's first epistle is one of the most pointed and poignant letters written exclusively to fellow believers. Following John's prologue, he immediately introduces his theme about believers and habitual sin. He writes:

Now this is the message we have heard from Him and declare to you: God is light, and there is absolutely no darkness in Him. If we say, "We have fellowship with Him," and walk in darkness, we are lying and are not practicing the truth. But if we walk in the light as He Himself is in the light, we have fellowship with one another, and the blood of Jesus His Son cleanses us from all sin. If we say, "We have no sin," we are deceiving ourselves, and the truth is not in us. If we confess our sins, He is faithful and righteous to forgive us our sins and to cleanse us from all unrighteousness. If we say, "We have not sinned," we make Him a liar, and His word is not in us. (1 John 1:5–10)

John clearly notes both sides of the equation. Believers must admit to sin; otherwise they are guilty of lying before God. Believers cannot, however, dwell in habitual sin ("walk in darkness") and claim to be Christians, because if we do, we are also guilty of lying to God.

The resolution of this dilemma is found in the beginning of the next chapter: "My little children, I am writing you these things so that you may not sin. But if anyone does sin, we have an advocate with the Father—Jesus Christ the righteous One. He Himself is the propitiation for our sins, and not only for ours, but also for those of the whole world" (1 John 2:1–2).

Christ, as our atonement, stands for us, and can break the bonds of those sins. He does so, not as our prosecutor, but as our defense attorney.

Continuously throughout the letter, we hear John warn believers that steady and habitual rebellion against God has heavy implications. One point the apostle John states is that habitual sin that does not produce grief might be a sign that the person who declares himself to be a "Christian" may in fact not be one.

> Everyone who commits sin also breaks the law; sin is
> the breaking of law. You know that He was revealed so
> that He might take away sins, and there is no sin in
> Him. Everyone who remains in Him does not sin;
> everyone who sins has not seen Him or known Him.
> Little children, let no one deceive you! The one who
> does what is right is righteous, just as He is righteous.
> The one who commits sin is of the Devil, for the Devil
> has sinned from the beginning. The Son of God was
> revealed for this purpose: to destroy the Devil's works.
> Everyone who has been born of God does not sin,
> because His seed remains in him; he is not able to sin,
> because he has been born of God. This is how God's
> children—and the Devil's children—are made evident.
> (1 John 3:4–10)

Does John mean that habitual sin is absolute proof that a person proves his pagan status by habitual sin? He does not seem to mean this to be such a "cut-and-dried" affirmative defense. Later in the same chapter, John invokes a softened conscience,

> Dear friends, if our hearts do not condemn [us] we have confidence before God, and can receive whatever we ask from Him because we keep His commands and do what is pleasing in His sight. Now this is His command: that we believe in the name of His Son Jesus Christ, and love one another as He commanded us. The one who keeps His commands remains in Him, and He in him. And the way we know that He remains in us is from the Spirit He has given us. (1 John 3:21–24)

God's presence in us is the internal proof, over and against the external evidences. We return to John's opening words, "If we say we do not sin we lie." John, under the inspiration of the Holy Spirit, seems to offer evidence that sin exists in the lives of both believers and nonbelievers.

What then is the consequence of sin without grief and penitence in the life of the believer? Is John arguing that a believer *cannot* come to the point of a hardened heart? We have a cryptic warning to the contrary. Please pay attention to the words explicit to this scenario: "There is sin that brings death. I am not saying he should pray about that. All unrighteousness is sin, and there is sin that does not bring death" (1 John 5:16–17).

Could the fate of Nabal be possible for a Christian? Can a Christian die of heart disease?

Symptoms and Diagnosis of Spiritual Hardening

In light of the previous warning from John, it would seem incumbent on the believer to remain sensitive to the Lord. Ask yourself these questions:

- Am I grieved by the sins that seem to ensnare me?
- Do I lay my heart concerns before God as the only one who can cure me?
- When was the last time I sensed the call of God in my life?
- Do I scoff at those who speak of hearing God's conviction and repent, as if I consider this a silly exercise?
- Do I find myself increasingly uncomfortable around strong believers and even mock them because their lives make me feel guilty?
- Do I often feel a twinge at the invitation hour and try to convince myself that stepping forward is an act of weakness? Do I wait for the feeling to subside?
- Do I justify my ongoing sin by saying, "This is the way everyone lives"?

A hardened heart, spiritually and physically, is no laughing matter. We do not accept the forgiveness of our sins purchased on Calvary and then scorn the one who calls us, convicts us, and challenges us. If you do not believe us, ask Nabal.

potato salad

Chapter 6

The Toxin of Bitterness: The Poison of Jealousy and Vengeance

Joab and Abner
2 Samuel 2–3

It all started so innocently—over potato salad.

As anyone in a country church can tell you, family recipes are guarded like Fort Knox gold. Many techniques and ingredients are passed down through generations and are considered classified. On deathbeds throughout the South, grandmothers who are preparing to meet Jesus whisper secret spices and combinations to their progeny, who in turn will pass them on to their children.

These recipes often make their way to church fellowship suppers. Competing bowls of potato salad, platters of fried chicken, and mounds of banana pudding stand side by side, and woe unto the unsuspecting pastor who chooses one potato salad over another! He had better be prepared to send out his resumé quickly, as he has grievously injured one family and given bragging rights to another.

That is what happened at Moriah Church.

On a particular Sunday, the church was to share in a meal following the morning service. A new pastor, not aware of the extenuating circumstances, did the requisite blessing before the meal and bragged on how the tables were bowlegged under the weight of such great food. As the new preacher, he was then invited, along with his family, to go first in line and fill up his plate.

Little did he know that this moment was more tenuous than a criminal background check!

Every woman was eyeing the preacher as he slowly made his way past the salads. Never one for green pea salad and cucumber slices, the pastor headed straight for the deviled eggs. While each of the eight varieties seemed, on the surface, to be exactly alike, this was deceptive. Beneath the thin layer of paprika lay eight different family recipes. He finally took a couple of deviled eggs off one plate and walked forward. The women all glanced at the woman who had made the chosen eggs. She just smiled, almost smugly, knowing that all eyes were on her.

The preacher then walked past the large serving bowls, which were filled with combinations of marshmallows, carrots, coconut, raisins, and pistachios. He wondered to himself, *Who would have thought that carrots would go well mixed with marshmallows?* Still, however, he had not come to the "testing table."

The testing table contained six different types of potato salad.

In our years as pastors, we have seen people walk past perfectly good bowls of potato salad, exclaiming and pointing, *"Who made this potato salad? I don't eat just anybody's potato salad."* It is serious business.

The preacher, without thinking, just grabbed the first bowl with a serving spoon in it. As all the women looked on, they watched the pastor unwittingly choose the potato salad made by the woman who had made the deviled eggs he had chosen. Now the fight was on.

Accusations began to fly.

Some charged the woman with moving the serving spoon to her bowl so the preacher would have to pick hers. Others accused her of stealing another woman's recipe, which obviously meant he did not choose her salad, but a facsimile of someone else's. Still others whispered that she had tipped off the pastor, telling him to pick her salad, which was seen as favoritism.

By the time the meal was over and women were carrying stoneware casserole dishes (with their names written in nail polish on the bottom) to their cars, people were taking sides. Within a year, the church was evenly divided. One half of the women sat on the left side of the church, and the other half sat on the right side of the church. Rarely did they even so much as glance at one another, though on occasion they would speak loudly enough that the others would hear, especially if their remarks were malicious enough.

Even the men were drawn into the conflict. Anyone who assumes that women are alone in the gossiping field has never been to a country store. The men sat on wooden barrels and spoke of hurt feelings and harried phone calls, and soon they were also picking sides. By the pastor's third anniversary, he had decided that this church was not even listening to him. The jealousy and bitterness had taken root. He would be gone by the next quarterly business meeting.

Bitterness is a serious thing.

The Root of Bitterness: Jealousy

As hard as we work to maintain warmth and love in a church fellowship, it can be destroyed very quickly. Nothing can tear apart a family, a friendship, or a fellowship as fast or as thoroughly as a fight brought on by jealousy. There is a reason why the writer of Hebrews calls bitterness a "root." Once it has taken hold, it spreads its evil tentacles into virtually every arena of life. It affects long-held friendships. It destroys marriages. It is a horror of epidemic proportions to behold. It is a deadly poison.

Jealousy and bitterness are twin diseases. One rarely sees one without anticipating the other. There is a reason why Job 5:2 says, "For anger kills a fool, and jealousy slays the gullible." It deceives the victim into believing he is justified in his sin. In short, we believe we have a right to be jealous, even if the Bible says it is a sin. Herein lies the problem. King Solomon, a man who struggled with many sinful impulses, understood that jealousy, wrath, and bitterness destroy the person from within. Notice his words in Proverbs and Ecclesiastes:

A tranquil heart is life to the body but jealousy is rottenness to the bones. (Prov. 14:30)

Fury is cruel, and anger is a flood, but who can withstand jealousy? (Prov. 27:4)

I saw that all labor and all skillful work is due to a man's jealousy of his friend. This too is futile and a pursuit of the wind. (Eccles. 4:4)

Can jealousy affect a church, as in the case of our opening illustration? Ask the apostle Paul, who warned the Corinthian fellowship: "For I fear that perhaps when I come I will not find you to be what I want, and I may not be found by you to be what you want; there may be quarreling, *jealousy,* outbursts of anger, selfish ambitions, slander, gossip, arrogance, and disorder" (2 Cor. 12:20).

We have a perfect example of the destructive effects of jealousy and bitterness in the war between Joab and Abner.

Joab and Abner: Kings in Combat (2 Sam. 2:8–32)

Few men have ever risen to such prominence as Joab and Abner. Abner was the commander of Saul's army. In the midst of the conflict with David's forces, the leader of David's forces was Joab. King Saul's death, as recorded in 1 Samuel 31, did not mean that his armies would surrender and the civil war would end. In fact, as commander of Saul's forces, Abner now had to make difficult decisions regarding his military without the benefit of his king.

Abner continued to fight, and he installed one of Saul's surviving sons as the new king over the northern regions. "Abner son of Ner, commander of Saul's army, took Saul's son Ish-bosheth and moved him to Mahanaim. He made him king over Gilead, Asher, Jezreel, Ephraim, Benjamin—over all Israel. Saul's son Ish-bosheth was 40 years old when he began his reign over Israel; he ruled for two years. The house of Judah, however, followed David" (2 Sam. 2:8–10).

This was not the wisest of decisions, especially since Ish-bosheth's name literally meant "son of Baal" or "man of shame." He was not the best man to lead the Israelites.

As the civil war progressed, both armies marched to the pool of Gibeon, where they took positions on opposite sides of the pool. The battle that ensued was fierce, with heavy casualties on both sides. In the end, however, Abner's forces were defeated by David's army, ruled by Joab (2 Sam. 2:14–17).

Running away in retreat after his defeat, Abner saw that one of Joab's brothers, Asahel, was chasing him. Though Abner continued to call to Asahel to stop chasing him, Asahel would not listen. Finally Abner turned and killed Asahel with his spear. Now the battle became intensely personal. The general of Saul's army had just killed the brother of the general of David's troops. Joab would have his revenge for the death of his brother, and he did not care how or when he would do it. He would even get his vengeance during a peacekeepers' summit.

Treachery at the Truce (2 Sam. 3:1–34)

Abner knew the kingdom of Saul was almost defeated. Fighting for a man who had been dead for two years was difficult enough. Add to this the fact that he had lost many men, and now he was engaged in a battle with Saul's son, his own king. Ish-bosheth (Saul's son) accused Abner of sleeping with his dead father's concubine. This allegation came more from Ish-bosheth's own jealousy than any fact, but Ish-bosheth brought it nonetheless.

Abner was indignant. Fighting a futile battle was one thing, since Abner had been loyal to King Saul. But it just added insult to injury when the king he had installed began to threaten him and make false accusations. Disgusted with the entire ordeal, Abner set about to make the peace and bring his troops to recognize David as the king over all of Israel. This long-standing war was going to come to an end, and Abner was going to broker the peace (2 Sam. 3:8–15).

Abner met with the elders of Israel, convincing them that God had given all the land and the leadership to King David. He even convinced the Benjaminites, who had united with him, to agree to surrender. On the appointed day, Abner and twenty of his men met King David in Hebron. David prepared a banquet for this former general who was now a peacemaker. At the banquet, Abner spoke to King David and all those who were in attendance: "Abner said to David, 'Let me now go and I will gather all Israel to my lord the king. They will make a covenant with you, and you will rule over all you desire.' So David dismissed Abner, and he went in peace" (2 Sam. 3:21).

Finally, the battle that had lasted far too long was almost over. Abner was dismissed by David and began his journey home to gather the vanquished forces.

Yet Joab, the general of David's army, still had unfinished business. When he arrived back from a raid, he discovered that David had met with Abner and had released him to go home. *This man killed my brother,* Joab must have thought, *and King David let him slip away.*

No amount of reasoning or rational thought could dissuade Joab. It is the same for those who are torn asunder by bitterness. He was going to get the justice for which he longed. Without telling David, Joab had Abner brought back to Hebron (2 Sam. 3:22–26).

Surely Abner must have assumed that Joab was going to confer with him over the surrender. Perhaps they would discuss the terms of peace. Whatever Abner thought, we will never know, because when he returned to Hebron, the Bible relates this chilling tale: "When Abner returned to Hebron, Joab pulled him aside to the middle of the gateway, as if to speak to him privately, and there Joab stabbed him in the stomach. So Abner died in revenge for the death of Asahel, Joab's brother" (2 Sam. 3:27).

David mourned, wept, and fasted. The people of Israel walked in the funeral procession to Abner's tomb. Yet no amount of mourning could undo the horrific deed. Even King David lamented that: "Then the king said to his soldiers, 'You must know that a great leader has fallen in Israel today. As for me, even though I am the anointed king, I have little power today. These men, the sons of Zeruiah, are too fierce for me. May the LORD repay the evildoer according to his evil'" (2 Sam. 3:38–39).

Abner had not just been killed by a knife wound; Abner was killed by bitterness.

The Nature of Bitterness

Bitterness is a bile so toxic that it can consume anyone who becomes afflicted by it. It obsesses your thoughts and devours your energy until you are emptied of any other motivation. It is poisonous and it is toxic, and it comes in two forms: bitterness from jealousy and bitterness from vengeance.

Bitterness that springs from jealousy comes from a deep place in a hardened heart. Even believers can become obsessed with jealousy. The jealous soul believes that others have been blessed more than they deserve. Jealous Christians also believe that they have been blessed less than they deserve. They feel abandoned and overlooked by God and man, and they develop a consuming resentment. It is a violation of the commandment in Exodus 20:17: "Do not covet your neighbor's house. Do not covet your neighbor's wife, his male or female slave, his ox or donkey, or anything that belongs to your neighbor."

How does this form of toxin develop in a believer? Imagine any of the following scenarios:

1. Your best friend becomes a deacon, and you did not receive enough votes.

2. Your best preacher friend gets invited to preach at a big conference and you do not.

3. Your seminary friend becomes pastor of the largest church in town, and you remain in a small church.

4. Your Bible study class remains small, but everyone is bragging about the class next door.

5. Your friend has prayers answered every week, it seems, and your list remains unchanged.

What is your response to these situations? Can you praise God with others as they celebrate his sovereign blessings, or do you reserve some small part of your heart for the "why not me" chorus? That small reservation, however seemingly insignificant, is called the "root of bitterness."

If left unchecked, it will take hold in your thought life, your prayer life, and your social life. You will begin to seek ways to avoid that person, even if he has been a good Christian friend for many years. Every time you look at him, you do not see a brother or sister with whom you have prayed, wept, and laughed. All you see is the person whom "God chose over you."

Ergun knew of a young couple many years ago who had struggled in vain for years to have a child. They were a godly couple who prayed together and remained faithful in spite of their disappointment. After subsequent miscarriages, a cloud slowly enveloped them. Joy and easy laughter were replaced by a grim smile and strained prayer requests. The situation became even worse when, one by one, their friends became pregnant and had children. It became so bad that friends even avoided talking about their pregnancies with the wife because she would grimace and clench her teeth in despair.

Toward the end, the couple avoided any contact with their friends, because it was just too much to bear. Though they were well-intentioned and genuine Christians, they had become infected with the poison of bitterness.

This type of bitterness does not stop at a jealousy toward others; it questions God himself. "Why did you choose to bless them?" The subsequent question can also be, "Why did you not choose me?" God's sovereign wisdom is now on trial, and eventually, the unrepentant, bitter Christian begins to question God's goodness. The prayer life dries up. Service becomes monotonous. The soul becomes disillusioned.

The natural by-product of this sinful obsession is cynicism. Cynicism is a hardened and withered response. Other people's joy and trust in God and men is seen as naïve, and the cynical Christian becomes a harbinger of doom. He usually uses sarcasm to communicate his bitter thoughts, but masks it in an attempt at bad humor. Sarcasm is often bitterness communicated with a smile.

Bitterness that springs from vengeance also comes from a deep place in a hardened heart. Christians who develop this type of bitterness seek unfulfilled justice, as in the case of Joab. Sins and crimes that go unpunished seem unfair to this person, and their mounting anger toward the one who seemingly "got away with it" ravages their heart.

The Christian who is consumed by this type of bitterness questions the goodness of God as well. "If you are God, then why did you allow this to happen?" The perpetrator begins to incinerate the heart of the person who has been wronged. The irony is, though the person who has been wronged is already a victim, he becomes a victim again by becoming a prisoner of the past transgression.

In Mac's first church after seminary, he inherited a church in the midst of a real struggle. During the period between pastors, the interim had led the church to rewrite its constitution. Few fights are ever as heated as those over a church constitution!

One particular deacon continued to push for the church to revisit a long-standing policy on divorce. Even though the church had long held to their particular position of divorce among the church leadership, and this deacon agreed with the policy, he still wanted the issue to be brought to the floor and voted on again.

For months this situation perplexed Pastor Mac. He could not understand why, if everyone seemed to be in agreement, this deacon insisted on raising the issue again in a church vote.

He soon discovered the reason. A young family had rejoined the church shortly after Mac had become pastor. He did not realize they were a blended family. This man, a business leader in the community, did not have any desire to be a deacon. However, he had recently become the new owner of the business in which the deacon worked. The deacon did not like the way the new owner was succeeding in the business.

To get back at his new boss, this deacon was using the church. Rather than following the biblical admonitions of fellowship, this deacon descended into a well of bitterness so deep that he was willing to use the sacred fellowship to carry out his revenge.

Get Rid of Bitterness Quickly

There is only one antidote to bitterness. The resolution is entirely in the hands of the victim. One must learn to both forgive and forget, and to do it quickly.

The devastating effect of bitterness is that it can consume the person who is afflicted with it. The person who seeks justice or is eaten up by jealousy does no harm to the person toward whom his anger is directed, except for affecting their relationship. It can stunt the Christian's growth, however, and will not allow him to enjoy God or his salvation.

Imagine this situation: You are driving down the road in a hurry to get to your job on time. Looking at your watch, you see that, if all things work together, you will make it on time without speeding—at least not too much. Suddenly you see that directly in your path is a big, old 1970s edition car. The type of car that has a million cubic inches under the hood and takes up a lane and a half.

Behind the wheel of this monster car is a little head. All you can see is the bald top of an elderly gentleman's head, along with his elderly wife in the seat beside him.

You honk your horn.

You swerve to get by them.

You flash your lights.

All this is to no avail. They are happily engaged in conversation and are oblivious to you and your situation. They are blissfully driving down the highway at 35 miles an hour, like the grand masters of the Rose Bowl parade.

You rant and you scream and you honk. Your mind fills with every imaginable evil thought. When you finally do pass them, you glare through the passenger side window. But again, they not only do not see you; neither do they see the twenty other cars that are now rushing to pass them.

Here is our question: While you are praying every imprecatory psalm on their heads, do you think it affects them in the least? While you get to your job and seethe with anger for three hours, do you think this hurts them?

Of course not.

They happily go on their way for breakfast, getting an early-bird special, or whatever else they do that day, while you fume away at your desk.

Welcome to the seeds of bitterness.

When you do not learn to forgive people for the wrongs they have done to you, you become a victim a second time. You become ensnarled in a cycle of hatred, poison, and bitterness that has no end and has no solution. This is why Jesus told the offended person to go to the one who has wronged him (Matt. 18:15). Notice how Paul compares jealousy with all the other sins of the flesh, commanding the churches of Galatia to avoid resentment at all costs:

> I say then, walk by the Spirit and you will not carry out
> the desire of the flesh. For the *flesh* desires what is
> against the Spirit, and the Spirit desires what is against
> the flesh; these are opposed to each other, so that you
> don't do what you want. But if you are led by the
> Spirit, you are not under the law. Now the works of the
> flesh are obvious: sexual immorality, moral impurity,

promiscuity, idolatry, sorcery, hatreds, strife, *jealousy,*
outbursts of anger, selfish ambitions, dissensions, fac-
tions, envy, drunkenness, carousing, and anything similar, about which I tell you in advance—as I told you
before—that those who practice such things will not
inherit the kingdom of God. But the *fruit of the Spirit* is
love, joy, peace, patience, kindness, goodness, faith, gentleness, self-control. Against such things there is no law.
Now those who belong to Christ Jesus have crucified
the flesh with its passions and desires. If we live by the
Spirit, we must also follow the Spirit. We must not
become *conceited, provoking one another, envying one another.*
(Gal. 5:16–26)

One Last Admonition

We must hasten to add one last piece of advice. Perhaps the
most difficult type of bitterness to conquer and the most insidious poison is this: *learning to forgive those who do not believe they need
forgiveness.*

Think about it for a moment. In seeking vengeance, we often
want the perpetrator to understand how much he has hurt us. He
has wronged us and has had a horrible impact on our lives, and
we wonder why God has not intervened and fixed the situation.

Perhaps you may have also followed the steps found in
Matthew 18, and gone to the person, and even brought a friend,
and sought some type of reconciliation. The most infuriating
component of this conflict would surely be if he does not believe
he has done anything wrong.

He does not want forgiveness.

He does not seek forgiveness.

He looks at you as if you are insane or weak.

He feels completely at ease with the horror that has befallen
you, and he might even act as if you had it coming to you.

How do you ever learn to forgive him?

The litany of people in this category is too long to mention. Loved ones who have sinned against you. People who have abused you. Crimes that have been perpetrated upon you. Perhaps the criminal has already died, and you do not feel you will ever get retribution.

Here is the difficult answer: *forgive them anyway.*

You have to release your hatred and desire for vengeance to God. Otherwise, your desire is (as difficult as this is to read and consider) to *be* God. That is why the Bible is replete with God's sayings, "Vengeance is mine." Retribution and judgment are in his divine and sovereign purview. As long as you continue harboring those feelings, you are intimating that God does not know what is best for you. You are acting as if you should be God!

Release these feelings to God. Allow him to handle the situation, and trust that his justice is far greater than yours. We know this is much more easily written than lived out, but it is the only solution. Forgiving is one thing. Forgiving those who don't want forgiveness is entirely another. It is the most difficult thing you can ever learn, but it will release your will to God and remove the poison of bitterness from your heart.

All bitterness, anger and wrath, insult and slander
must be removed from you,
along with all wickedness. (Eph. 4:31)
See to it that no one falls short of the grace of God
and that no root of bitterness springs up,
causing trouble and by it, defiling many.
(Heb. 12:15)

Chapter 7

Gluttony: Always Full; Ever Empty

The Pharisees in Confrontation with Jesus
Matthew 23:1–39

How Great I Art: The Legacy of Bill

You could see him coming a mile away.

Bill was one of those rare Christians who had the capacity to both infuriate and amuse at the same time. He practiced this gift every Sunday in church. Few people took him very seriously, and yet when he would finish a conversation with them, they would brood and stew for the rest of the day. Bill was a modern-day Pharisee.

Every Sunday he wore his Sunday school pins. For those unaware of this particular tradition, in years gone by churches would hand out pins for those people who had an unbroken chain of Sunday school attendance. Upon completing one year without missing a single Sunday, the pastor would recognize the person in the service and give him a pin. The person who did not miss for a second year would receive an additional pin that would link to the first one. After a while, the pins would dangle from the original one like a chain.

Bill's chain was long, and he never forgot to wear it.

Neither did he neglect to point it out to anyone, even in casual conversation. It would be an understatement to say that he was proud of those pins. He relished them.

He had this amazing gift to let someone know how holy he was, even in the most benign discussion. He often began sentences with,

"You know, this morning, in my third prayer time, I was thinking . . ."

"Yesterday, while I was memorizing the book of Jeremiah . . ."

"Of course, anyone who is spiritual knows . . ."

"Of course, you know the Greek word for that term actually means . . ."

You get the picture? Few people were so impressed with the depth of their own personal faith as Bill.

His capacity to anger other Christians was equally renowned. He was the master of giving the backhanded rebuke. A particular example that had become legendary came from his Sunday school class. For as long as anyone could remember, Bill had taught a class for men in the basement of the church. Each Sunday he would take prayer requests at the beginning of class. On the Sunday in question, one member had mentioned that he had seen a college football player break his leg during an exciting game. The other members of the class began to discuss the game and the injury in question. Bill sat stoically as they briefly conferred, and it was obvious he did not approve of the prayer request. Finally, one of the men asked Bill if he had seen the injury.

With a withering gaze, Bill replied, "No, we do not watch television. We are a Christian household."

Discussion ended, and the silence in the room hung in the air like a foul odor.

Although Bill had an unblemished Sunday school attendance record, the same could not be said for his worship attendance. In fact, Bill was famous for often leaving after Sunday school to go home. This was especially the case if he had been in a tiff with the pastor. If he did not feel that the particular sermon series was "challenging enough" for him, he would leave after his class. He had done it to a variety of pastors, but it never ceased to infuriate every one of them. When he was asked about his practice, he would lower his glasses to the edge of his nose, snort about the "lack of real meat" in the sermons, and then continue about the paucity of true biblical preaching these days.

Bill also had the habit of coming to church directly after work each Wednesday. The church had long offered a meal before the Wednesday night activities, and the fellowship hall was usually buzzing by 6:00 PM. Tables were filled with missions teachers, youth, children, workers, and the like. The price of the meal was very reasonable, and it was supposed to give the members a chance to eat before coming to various Wednesday night activities.

It had been especially successful in helping the attendance in the pastor's Wednesday night class. Many people would be so tired and hungry after work that they would go straight home and miss the class. Since the church had been providing the meal, attendance had skyrocketed. The hard-working kitchen staff labored diligently to provide good meals, and their tireless efforts were obviously successful.

Except in the case of Bill.

Bill would always come early, and he would almost always be the first person in line. He greeted the women warmly and complimented them on the food. He would be seated at one of the round tables to eat, and he always entered conversations with those around him. He inevitably lingered after he had finished as well and slowly sipped coffee from a Styrofoam cup.

Then Bill would go home.

He never attended the Wednesday night prayer meeting and Bible study.

He never worked in the children's missions programs.

He never volunteered to help with the youth or even the nursery.

He just went home.

It never ceased to enrage the pastor. The pastor would rarely eat the meal, choosing instead to look at his notes one last time before the study. He would, however, walk through the fellowship hall and greet people. He would shake hands, kiss babies, and listen to prayer requests. And almost every Wednesday, he would see Bill out of the corner of his eye, walking out the door toward the church parking lot.

At first, the pastor would hasten to greet Bill as well and engage him in conversation. But as the years wore on, Bill did not even flinch when the pastor gently requested his attendance in the sanctuary. He would just smile and nod, without giving a response. To make matters worse, he became a type of "Pied Piper" for others who wanted to eat without the burden of actually attending or helping. They would all sit at the same table, even lingering sometimes far past the hour when all others had gone to the various ministries and events. The men and women in charge of cleaning up the fellowship hall would cast glances at this cadre of non-attenders, but they seemed unaware of the dirty looks they were getting.

Like we said, Bill was a modern-day Pharisee, and he was infectious.

The Cliché Is Wrong: Hypocrites in the Midst

Perhaps it has become a well-worn adage to say that hypocrites can be found in the church. The term *hypocrisy* has almost lost its meaning, given its usage in our culture. However, we believe that the modern use of the term is actually far removed from the biblical intent. Odd as it may sound, true hypocrisy is actually far worse than we have expected.

Imagine a coffee house setting, complete with young philosophy students, lounging on couches. They casually watch the television when a reporter speaks of the breaking news story: A prominent minister has been caught in a public scandal, and he is now facing a police investigation and criminal charges.

The students smirk at the screen and say, "Another hypocrite falls."

This is how the world defines a hypocrite. He is a Christian, or a minister, who spends his time judging others, but is secretly carrying on in some lasciviousness. He is guilty of the very transgressions he so loudly condemns. To the average non-believer, the hypocrite is a justification for their belief that everyone "sins," and that the truly authentic people are those who do so in the open. It justifies their nonjudgmental position of "live-and-let-live," regardless of what they encounter. The hypocrite, who preaches one thing but lives another, is proof positive of the fallacy of Christianity. It is now part of our cultural landscape.

It may be a variation of hypocrisy, but it is not the worst kind. Jesus saw a far worse manifestation of hypocrisy. His definition of hypocrisy inverts the previous definition entirely.

His condemnation of the Pharisees was a pointed reference *not* to those who had fallen into public sin and scorn, but rather to those who were living lives beyond reproach! They were publicly pious and privately chaste, and yet Jesus reserved his most scathing rebuke for them. To our Lord, the worst form of hypocrisy was to follow the letter of the law, but not the spirit.

Why?

That precise question is the purpose of this chapter.

True hypocrisy is actually a heart condition rather than a disease of the "flesh." It is a symptom of the more infectious disease of gluttony. The Pharisees had studied the minutiae of the law down to exacting and painstaking detail, but had missed the point altogether. To further the analogy, they had eaten at the trough of Judaic teachings but had digested very little. They had much information (that would be the food) but very few

nutrients (that would be truth). In short, they had outward obedience, but no inner devotion.

Jesus and the Pharisees: Inverting the Definition

Though all four of the Gospels detail Christ's confrontations
with the Pharisees, none is more pointed than Matthew. He mentions this Jewish sect twenty-eight times, and one begins to see a
trend develop in Matthew's narrative. At each altercation, the
Pharisees are shown to be attempting to catch Jesus in a public
conundrum. They pose a question that they assume he cannot
answer, because regardless of his answer, he will either deny the
truth of Scripture or condemn some downtrodden sector of the
people who were following him.

In each instance, Jesus rebuffs their efforts, and not only
answers with profundity, but he also exposes their hypocrisy.
True hypocrisy is Pharisaical hypocrisy: they follow the letter of
the law but ignore the core meaning and purpose of the law. They
were externally pious and internally corrupt. They were true
hypocrites. They were legalists.

As we follow Matthew's narration, we can see Jesus becoming increasingly angered by their pseudo-piety until he con-
fronts their maliciousness head on in Matthew 23. At each
meeting, the Pharisees ask questions they assume Jesus could
not answer.

Jesus, Why Do You Eat with Sinners? (Matt. 9:10–13)

As Jesus was at the table, eating with Matthew's friends, the
Pharisees approached and actually asked the question of his disciples. "While He was reclining at the table in the house, many
tax collectors and sinners came as guests to eat with Jesus and
His disciples. When the Pharisees saw this, they asked His disciples, 'Why does your Teacher eat with tax collectors and sinners?'" (Matt. 9:10–11).

Jesus' response was one of profound clarity. He said, "Those
who are well don't need a doctor, but the sick do. Go and learn

what this means: I desire mercy and not sacrifice. For I didn't come to call the righteous, but sinners" (Matt. 9:12–13).

His citation of Hosea 6:6 pointed to his purpose and mission and also pointed to one of their glaring weaknesses. As part of their outward ritualistic piety, they had isolated themselves from the very people they were supposed to reach.

Jesus, Why Do You Defy Sabbath Law? (Matt. 12:1–8)

In their second attempt at publicly rebuking Jesus, the Pharisees caught him and the disciples eating some grain during the Sabbath. Have you ever wondered why the Pharisees did not accuse Jesus and the disciples of theft? Was Jesus guilty of stealing, since they were eating grain that was not their own? Surely the Pharisees were aware that the law did make provision for eating on a journey. Deuteronomy 23:25 speaks specifically to this situation: "When you enter your neighbor's standing grain, you may pluck heads of grain with your hand, but you must not put a sickle to your neighbor's grain."

Regardless, this was not the major offense that so inflamed the Pharisees. They rebuked the Lord and his disciples for actually eating on the Sabbath, which was not a violation of the Old Testament law, but rather a violation of the hundreds of traditions the Jewish leaders had developed. Do you understand the implication? The Pharisees were not accusing Jesus of violating the Scriptures. They were accusing him of violating their traditions.

Jesus' response was again focused on the major emphasis of Scripture: God cares more about inner righteousness than about outer obedience. He cited the story of David, found in 1 Samuel 21:1–6. King David ate the bread that was specifically reserved for the priests, according to Levitical law (Lev. 24:5–9). Jesus was asking them: Did David violate the law? He also noted that the priests entered the temple on the Sabbath.

He then emphatically made his point: "But I tell you that something greater than the temple is here! If you had known what this means: I desire mercy and not sacrifice, you would not have condemned the innocent. For the Son of Man is Lord of the Sabbath" (Matt. 12:6–8).

Jesus, Can You Do Good Things in the Wrong Way? (Matt. 12:9–13)

Never one to shirk from attack, Jesus then entered the synagogue, and the Pharisees attempted to trap him there. If you are the Lord of the Sabbath, they seemed to imply, Can you do something that violates your own law, even if it is for a good reason? Can you heal on the Sabbath? Jesus responded: "What man among you, if he had a sheep that fell into a pit on the Sabbath, wouldn't take hold of it and lift it out? A man is worth far more than a sheep, so it is lawful to do good on the Sabbath" (Matt. 12:11–12).

Jesus noted that the Pharisees were more willing to rescue an animal on the Sabbath than a person because of their ritualistic traditions.

Jesus, Can You Show Us a Sign? (Matt. 12:38–42; 16:1–8)

Having heard Jesus claim to be God ("Son of Man"), and having watched Jesus subsequently heal a paralytic, the Pharisees then asked Jesus for proof—a miracle or manifestation—that he truly was who he said he was. Were they thinking perhaps of the cloud of fire by night, proving God's presence to the Israelites? Were they willing to believe, if only he would show them?

They were missing the entire message! Jesus was compelling men to faith. Faith, as we know, does not walk by sight. Ritual, tradition, and legalism walk by sight. He did not mince words:

But He answered them, "An evil and adulterous generation demands a sign, but no sign will be given to it except the sign of the prophet Jonah. For as Jonah was in the belly of the great fish three days and three nights, so the Son of Man will be in the heart of the earth three days and three nights. The men of Nineveh will stand up at the judgment with this generation and condemn it, because they repented at Jonah's proclamation; and look—something greater than Jonah is here! The queen of the south will rise up at the judgment with this generation and condemn it, because she came from the ends of the earth to hear the wisdom of Solomon; and look—something greater than Solomon is here!" (Matt. 12:39–42)

Jesus, Why Do You Break Our Traditions? (Matt. 15:1–9)

The Pharisees were now pledged to stop Jesus at all costs. If he was truly teaching the people that inner faith is more important than outer evidence, then he was disrupting their entire system. Approaching Jesus, they saw that his disciples did not ceremonially wash their hands before they ate. After the Jews had returned from the Babylonian captivity, the rabbis had developed an elaborate system of prescriptions for everyday life. This collection of traditions, which would come to be called the Mishnah, was as important to the Pharisees as the actual Word of God itself.

Jesus answered by showing that their traditions were a violation of God's commandments because they went further than even God did. His rebuke was not without a point, as he said: "Hypocrites! Isaiah prophesied correctly about you when he said: These people honor Me with their lips, but their heart is far from Me. They worship Me in vain, teaching as doctrines the commands of men" (Matt. 15:7–9).

Jesus, Can We Amend the Bible with Our Traditions? (Matt. 19:1–9)

Now the Pharisees thought they had cornered Jesus. Two Jewish schools of thought had disagreed on how to interpret the teaching on divorce from Deuteronomy 24:1–4. The school of Shammai held that divorce was only acceptable for reasons of marital infidelity. The school of Hillel (60 BC–AD 20) had modified this to mean that any type of infidelity was grounds for divorce. Thus, if a woman burned the dinner, then she was being unfaithful to her position in the home. Her husband could divorce her.

They were asking Jesus on which side of the argument he stood.

Jesus responded that they had both missed the original intent for marriage, turning it into a series of conditions and contracts. Thus, he was not on either side, since they were both attempting to modify God's teaching. They were more interested in "divorce papers" (Matt. 19:7) than two being of one flesh.

Jesus, Do We Obey God or Men? (Matt. 22:15–22)

The Pharisees felt they could trap Jesus into committing the crime of treason and sedition. If he was so "heavenly minded," they reasoned, surely he would scoff at giving anything to the government. If he taught that paying taxes was illegal, then Rome would imprison him immediately.

His answer amazed them. He simply told them to "give back to Caesar the things that are Caesar's and to God the things that are God's" (22:21). Jesus did not see any inherent contradiction between serving God faithfully and being a citizen.

Jesus, What Is the Most Important Rule to Follow? (Matt. 22:34–40)

Throughout his entire ministry on earth, Jesus had rebuffed any attempt by the Pharisees to equate their own rules and rituals with the Word of God. Finally, they asked him which of the commandments was most important. Were they hoping for him to emphasize murder over lying? Were they attempting to get Jesus to pick one biblical sin over the other, effectively establishing a hierarchy of sin? Which commandment would Jesus say? Adultery? Disobedience to one's parents?

Though the Pharisees were hoping to catch Jesus in an unsolvable dilemma, he once again trumped them. Jesus cited the fundamental call of God in Deuteronomy 6:4–9, called the Sh'ema Israel. The Lord also showed the hidden component of the love of God. Loving God also means loving the mankind he created.

He said to him, "Love the Lord your God with all your heart, with all your soul, and with all your mind. This is the greatest and most important commandment. The second is like it: Love your neighbor as yourself. All the Law and the Prophets depend on these two commandments." (Matt. 22:37–40)

Jesus Turns the Tables (Matt. 22:41–46)

Having thwarted their feeble attempts at trapping him, Jesus finally asked the Pharisees a question that they thought, on the surface, was a simple one. He asked: "What do you think about the Messiah? Whose Son is He?" (Matt. 22:42).

It was a relatively easy question and certainly so for a group that had studied prophecy their entire lives. They responded quickly, "David's."

It was at this juncture that Jesus completely turned the tables on the Pharisees. He exposed both the logic of his claims of divinity, and the folly of their hatred of him. "He asked them, 'How is it then that David, inspired by the Spirit, calls Him "Lord": The Lord declared to my Lord, "Sit at My right hand until I put Your enemies under Your feet"? If David calls Him "Lord," how then can the Messiah be his Son?'" (Matt. 22:43–45).

Why would David call his own son, his own progeny, "Lord"? Could it be that the Pharisees had studied the intricacies of the prophecies but had missed the message altogether? Apparently so, because Matthew 22:46 notes, "No one was able to answer Him at all, and from that day no one dared to question Him anymore."

Game. Set. Match.

Jesus Turns Up the Heat (Matt. 23:1–39)

Our Lord had finally had enough. Brimming with righteous indignation, Jesus reserved his most pointed holy anger for those who were perpetrators of true hypocrisy. They professed to be wise, but he had shown them to be fools. They had professed to be holy, and he had shown them to be hypocrites. In quick fashion, Jesus condemned these pseudo-pious practitioners of the law.

His clear indictment of these gluttons is found in Matthew 23:3: "Don't do what they do, because they don't practice what they teach." This form of hypocrisy, this spiritual gluttony, where the falsely pious only receive but rarely give, was reviled and rejected by Jesus:

> They tie up heavy loads that are hard to carry and put them on people's shoulders, but they themselves aren't willing to lift a finger to move them. They do everything to be observed by others: They enlarge their phylacteries and lengthen their tassels. They love the place of honor at banquets, the front seats in the synagogues, greetings in the marketplaces, and to be called "Rabbi" by people. But as for you, do not be called "Rabbi," because you have one Teacher, and you are all brothers. Do not call anyone on earth your father, because you have one Father, who is in heaven. And do not be called masters either, because you have one Master, the Messiah. The greatest among you will be your servant. Whoever exalts himself will be humbled, and whoever humbles himself will be exalted.
> (Matt. 23:4–12)

Then in short order, Jesus outlined the judgment of the Pharisees in eight separate indictments. He completely inverted everything upon which the Pharisees had built their lives.

1. *Jesus condemns their isolation.* "But woe to you, scribes and Pharisees, hypocrites! You lock up the kingdom of heaven from people. For you don't go in, and you don't allow those entering to go in" (Matt. 23:13).

2. *Jesus condemns their ritualism.* "Woe to you, scribes and Pharisees, hypocrites! You devour widows' houses and make

long prayers just for show. This is why you will receive a harsher punishment" (Matt. 23:14).

3. *Jesus condemns their proselyting.* "Woe to you, scribes and Pharisees, hypocrites! You travel over land and sea to make one proselyte, and when he becomes one, you make him twice as fit for hell as you are!" (Matt. 23:15).

4. *Jesus condemns their love of money.* "Woe to you, blind guides, who say, 'Whoever takes an oath by the sanctuary, it means nothing. But whoever takes an oath by the gold of the sanctuary is bound by his oath'" (Matt. 23:16).

5. *Jesus condemns their lack of mercy.* "Woe to you, scribes and Pharisees, hypocrites! You pay a tenth of mint, dill, and cumin, yet you have neglected the more important matters of the law — justice, mercy, and faith. These things should have been done without neglecting the others. Blind guides! You strain out a gnat, yet gulp down a camel!" (Matt. 23:23–24).

6. *Jesus condemns their external legalism.* "Woe to you, scribes and Pharisees, hypocrites! You clean the outside of the cup and dish, but inside they are full of greed and self-indulgence! Blind Pharisee! First clean the inside of the cup, so the outside of it may also become clean" (Matt. 23:25–26).

7. *Jesus condemns their emptiness.* "Woe to you, scribes and Pharisees, hypocrites! You are like whitewashed tombs, which appear beautiful on the outside, but inside are full of dead men's bones and every impurity. In the same way, on the outside you seem righteous to people, but inside you are full of hypocrisy and lawlessness" (Matt. 23:27–28).

8. *Jesus condemns their lack of repentance and guilt.* "Woe to you, scribes and Pharisees, hypocrites! You build the tombs of the prophets and decorate the monuments of the righteous, and you say, 'If we had lived in the days of our fathers, we wouldn't have taken part with them in shedding the prophets' blood.' You therefore testify against yourselves that you are sons of those who murdered the prophets. Fill up, then, the measure of your fathers' sins!" (Matt. 23:29–32).

So Jesus, How Do You Really Feel About Pharisees?

As if his series of condemnations were not enough, Jesus put the final nail in the coffin when he addressed the Pharisees in languages they surely had not heard before:

Snakes! Brood of vipers! How can you escape being condemned to hell? This is why I am sending you prophets, sages, and scribes. Some of them you will kill and crucify, and some of them you will flog in your synagogues and hound from town to town. So all the righteous blood shed on the earth will be charged to you, from the blood of righteous Abel to the blood of Zechariah, son of Berechiah, whom you murdered between the sanctuary and the altar. I assure you: All these things will come on this generation! (Matt. 23:33–36)

Enter the Modern Pharisees: Symptoms of Gluttony

If you have finished reading the preceding pages and wondered, *What does this have to do with me or my church,* then hang on. This chapter is more than just a historical study of one of the first-century Jewish sects. It is more than just a biblical study of the series of "woes" with which Jesus denounced the group.

Pharisees are alive and well and living in your church. Their symptoms are so faint, and their infection so subtle that you might begin to show the signs of their infiltration before you know it. You may have even read this far and thought happily, *Well, I am grateful that I do not recognize any Pharisees or gluttons in my fellowship.*

We invite you to look again at Jesus' opening words in Matthew 23. These are the most glaring of indicators:

- They did not practice what they preached.
  (Matt. 23:1–3)
- They placed heavy loads on the shoulders of others but carried nothing themselves (Matt. 23:4).

- They prominently displayed the symbols of their false devotion (Matt. 23:5).
- They always sat in the places of honor in the synagogue (Matt. 23:6).
- They loved to be greeted with titles of holiness (Matt. 23:7).

On the surface, perhaps you do not recognize any of these symptoms in your fellowship. Since we do not wear phylacteries or tassels, perhaps the point is lost on you, but allow us to translate the principles within Jesus' words.

The Pharisees were old-school legalists.

They loved the law but did not love mercy. They were quick to condemn, slow to forgive, and suffered from an insufferable superiority complex. They condemned others who did not show the signs of holiness as they did, and they always measured holiness by outward appearances. They knew the law, but rarely did they use it to encourage others or to point to hope. They used the law to condemn and separate. They knew everything in the law, but ironically, they knew nothing about the law.

They were gluttons. They had eaten everything and yet absorbed nothing. Like the morbidly obese man who eats nothing but junk food, they were unhealthy because they hungered and thirsted for nothing. They were satisfied with a substitute for true Bread. Christ's indictment of the Pharisees was a profound one. They were guilty of the worst kind of hypocrisy. They lived a pious and separate life, so outwardly men could find no fault in them. Yet they were inwardly empty and dead.

The Glutton's Superiority Complex: Legalism

As if these indicators are not enough to convince you that gluttony, the disease of the Pharisees, is a malignant one, then perhaps you will recognize one of the most frustrating dimensions of a true Pharisee: superiority complex. They were experts in the art and science of legalism, and they felt quite proud of themselves.

Please do not miss this point.

We are not espousing a type of Christianity that mocks separation or lives of holiness. Indeed, the Bible is full of admonitions to a holy life marked by distinct choices. But one of the most meaningful principles you may draw from this study is the contrast between the true Christianity of the Bible and the legalism of

 the Pharisees. It can be summarized: *Christianity is concerned with your looking more like Christ. Legalists want you to look more like them.*

This was the mark of the Pharisees. Anyone who did not look like them, act like them, talk like them, and smell like them did not pass their personal litmus test of "true" piety. They measured by external indicators, not internal transformations. Most importantly, legalists use a telling standard for holiness—themselves. Not Christ, but themselves. They will rebuke you immediately when you fall short of the standard they themselves have set for holiness. They feel superior to you because they stand closest to their own standard.

The Marks of a Gluttonous Pharisee

One of the most difficult assertions in this chapter is the discovery that it is virtually impossible to cure a Pharisee. This is not to say that they are beyond redemption, but the nature of the disease itself precludes cure. To be spiritually cured of any malady of the heart, one must *want* to be cured. One must be *willing* to repent. Pharisees do not want a cure, because they do not believe they *need* a cure. In their minds not only are they not sick or infectious; they are more healthy than *you.*

It is possible, however, to diagnose and recognize the symptoms of a gluttonous Pharisee, if for no other reason than to avoid them. Using Jesus' denunciations in Matthew 23, we can deduce certain indicators of spiritual gluttony.

A Pharisee Has an Unteachable Spirit (Matt. 23:7)

The Pharisees loved to be called "Rabbi," which means "teacher." They did not want to learn, and neither did they believe they needed to learn. They were God's little "know-it-alls." They were ready to contradict anyone who disagreed with their position, and often, in confrontations, used this phrase: "Oh, I used to be just like you until I matured."

These were the men, like Bill in our opening illustration, who left after Sunday school, because they did not believe the pastor was "deep enough" for them. Never mind that all of their learning did not result in actual service. The knowledge they had was enough for them.

In one of Ergun's churches, he had a deacon who could wax eloquent on every doctrine under the sun. He had garnered many certificates from Discipleship Training and was obviously well versed in theological terminology. The problem was, he never went on visitation, never helped in evangelism, and never attended Sunday nights or Wednesday nights. When Ergun confronted him, he would simply shrug his shoulders and then launch into his justification. He used the sovereignty of God (which he called the "doctrines of grace") to justify his lack of involvement in any outreach of the church. No amount of reasoning, logic, or even prayer could convince him otherwise. In his mind, he had outgrown the need for such activities. He was "deep."

In truth, he wasn't deep; he had sunk to the bottom. He was unteachable.

A Pharisee Shows a Lack of Forgiveness and Mercy (Matt. 23:4)

When one becomes ensnarled in legalism, mercy and restoration go out the window. They are replaced with stern judgments and solemn warnings. Jesus reached out to the Samaritan woman at the well in John 4. In the minds of the Pharisees, the woman was beyond redemption. She had three strikes against her: (1) she had been married many times, (2) she was a Samaritan, and (3) she was a woman. In the Pharisees' mind, the Samaritan woman deserved a punitive judgment, not mercy or restoration.

Jesus, of course, inverted this process. He did not ignore her sin or even let her justify it. He simply restored the woman and loved her in spite of her wretched life and choices. While others were prepared to cast stones at the woman caught in adultery, Jesus did not, and neither did he think any of them were qualified to do so.

Consider the people in your church. Do the strong and active members minister to society's "outcasts," or do they use them as illustrations for their own superiority? Do they ignore those who have sinned and made poor choices, or do they embrace them? *Our Lord is the God of the second chance. Many of our fellowships are churches of the first strike.*

Consider the fact that many people who have suffered through the ravages of painful divorce turn to their church. They look to their "family" for help and hope. They are devastated. The children are torn, the family unit is broken, and their hearts are heavy.

Does your church embrace them and love them through the healing they can find in Christ, or do you brand them with a new "Scarlet Letter"—the scarlet "D"? Are they shunned in the hallways? Do they hear whispers in the sanctuary? Are they scorned and removed from any service? Have you treated them as if they have committed the unforgivable sin?

Pharisees Choose Preference Over Principle (Matt. 23:6)

Remember, Jesus noted that the Pharisees wanted the best seats in the synagogue. They wanted the best seats at the banquet. This was not just for prominence. This was for position. They had grown accustomed to being honored in the best seats. They were comfortable with their positions, and they were happy with the arrangements.

Anyone or anything that threatened that arrangement was a danger to them and their comfort zone.

We often note that there is a measure of hypocrisy in evangelical churches when we speak of Roman Catholicism. Evangelical pastors in evangelical churches often speak scornfully of the ritual, pomp, and circumstance in Catholic liturgy. This ritualism is a preference, to be sure. It is not prescribed in

Scripture. This formalism does have the tendency to drain any life from worship.

But Baptists do the same thing.

We evangelicals have our own liturgy, our own formalism, and our own ritualism: it is called the bulletin. If you do not believe us, try switching the order of service next Sunday, and then brace yourself. The outcry will be formidable.

The reason for this is that a Pharisee does not understand the difference between the biblical principles found throughout the Bible and the preferences they have developed over time.

Let us illustrate. A principle of Scripture is that a person must dress respectfully in church. Paul admonished the Christians to dress in a way that does not distract from worship or cause another person to lust.

Wearing a suit and tie is a preference. Now, it is a preference we do not mind at times, but it is a preference nonetheless. Nowhere does the Bible say that we should wear a long, narrow strip of fabric that chokes us half the time!

See the difference?

What preference do you hold in equal esteem with biblical principles? Times of worship? The early church met daily. Order of worship? They sang and preached.

Please do not misunderstand us. We are not mocking traditions. Traditions can be good if they enable us to carry out the call of God most effectively. However, there is a problem with *traditionalism.*

Traditionalism is actually the worship of the "way we have always done it." It is held in equal weight as the Bible, often because that is the way our parents or grandparents did it. As it often has been said: *Tradition is the living faith of dead men. It has been passed down as an effective means of worship and service. Traditionalism is the dead faith of living men. It is the Pharisees' comfort zone.*

Pharisees Always Choose Isolation Over Insulation (Matt. 23:13)

Jesus rebuked the Pharisees for keeping the gospel from the very people whom they were commanded to share it with. He said: "You lock up the kingdom of heaven from people. For you don't go in, and you don't allow those entering to go in."

Their justification for such actions? To come in contact with the pagan world would defile them and make them unclean. Therefore, they had developed an elaborate system that enabled them to avoid all contact with people. They became a "holy huddle." They used the doctrine of "separation" to lead them to "isolation."

How does your church respond to visitors? How do you respond to the unwashed masses you encounter? There is a movement in contemporary Christianity that espouses the removal of all contact with the world and thus proclaims a spiritual "cleanliness." In fact, those who have no contact with the lost world have abdicated their responsibility. Their churches have become the "sepulchers" of which Christ spoke. They are ceremonially clean but spiritually ineffective.

Chapter 8

Manic Depression: Ain't No Mountain High Enough

The Apostle Peter
Matthew 26:31–75

The Invitation Dance

In evangelical churches, the invitation is the last act of the worship service where people are invited to respond to God's Word. We do business with God, responding to the call to salvation, decision, surrender to Christian service, or rededication. We pray for our lost loved ones or leave our burdens at the altar, asking God to intercede in our lives.

In the average evangelical church, sadly, the invitation is the time to zip up our coats, put the bulletin in the Bible, and find our keys, while the organist and pianist play through three verses of

"I Have Decided to Follow Jesus." On occasion, people have the courage to step forward and deal with eternal matters. In those instances, the pastor admonishes everyone to bow their heads and close their eyes as others make decisions. Some people in every church use the opportunity to do what we call the "invitation sneak peek," peering through barely splayed fingers to see who is coming down the aisle. In any case, it rarely takes longer than just a few moments, and then a final prayer is uttered, and the people are dismissed.

Not at the church that Harrison attended. For this church, the invitation was a *prolonged* affair.

For as long as anyone could remember, Harrison would come forward at the invitation. Every invitation. It mattered not if the service was a Sunday morning, Sunday night, or a week-night during the revival meeting. Harrison always came forward.

Interestingly, it also did not matter what was the focus of the service or sermon. Sermons on family, love, forgiveness, patriotism, wrath, and even senior saints seemed to touch his heart. Harrison always came forward. Some people even qui-etly joked (though never to Harrison's face) that if the pastor preached on tithing, Harrison would be the first down the aisle as well.

His reasons for coming forward were never clear, but his emotions often were. At times, he stepped out cheerfully and stepped to the altar like a child approaches a parent after open-ing his Christmas presents. He could almost be overheard, thanking God for various blessings. Other times, Harrison was crying as he walked forward, passing the pastor and kneeling at the altar. His weeping would often become uncontrollable, and the pastor would have to speak over his lamentations. The one constant was that at the invitation hour, Harrison was coming forward, and the congregation would sing at least ten stanzas.

Please understand, the church was not cynical or hardened to Harrison. Not at all. They just understood that, well, that was Harrison. His personality was such that, given the day and the hour, he was either witnessing the incredible, miraculous wonders of God, or he was within scant moments of devastating failure. To be sure, Harrison was a spiritual manic-depressive.

His emotional lurches were not limited to the altar call. In everyday life, Harrison's emotions ran the gamut. On certain days, he floated into the church, happily singing hymns and greeting every person in sight. He would share praises during the prayer meeting that exalted God for his intervention in various affairs, even down to the smallest detail. He testified during "praise time" in the services, standing to share tremendous stories of God's miracle-working power. During these periods, he was on top of the world.

However, at other times, Harrison could not be more despondent. His world, at least through his eyes, was collapsing. He would keep people on the phone for hours as he shared his doubts, pains, and burdens. Two or three members remembered times when he was almost suicidal, lamenting the hopelessness of his condition.

Harrison was a classic case of spiritual manic depression.

Harrison was also the associate pastor at the church.

Harrison's Forefather: The Apostle Peter

Though you may be shocked by the previous illustration, it would do you well to know that Harrison is not alone. Scan your congregation. Virtually every church has one or two people who live on mountains or in valleys. Often they traverse them on the same day. Some might call them emotionally unstable or chalk it up to some chemical imbalance. Certainly we do not want to discount such diagnoses, especially in an age of medical advances for those who seem to be controlled by their external circumstances.

However, for many others, their emotional roller coaster is not a chemical or medical condition; it is a spiritual problem. They cannot control their emotional levels, and they consume the time of staff and members alike. They are vocal and they are needy. They can also be dangerous.

Churches become especially susceptible to the effects of a spiritually unstable person when they commit the cardinal sin of church work: They put a spiritually manic-depressive person in a position of leadership. It usually happens when the pastor or leadership team encounters the person at a high point in his journey. He is positive. He is strong. He is a visionary. He has great dreams and can speak of the accomplishment of amazing works for the Lord.

Days later, however, this same person can become despondent, almost to the point of total despair. He fails to follow up on plans. He misses his own meetings. He allows major events to collapse under the weight of his "dark night." When the church recognizes the pattern of enthusiastic beginnings and subsequent failures, it is often too late. The damage has been done.

We would submit that the problem is far more epidemic than you would imagine. Many more people are unstable in their emotional levels, in the pew, than in the leadership. These are the people who devour your time. They become dependent on your biblical wisdom. If your advice helps them through a crisis, then their dependence is even deeper and more cemented. They become the "puppies" who follow you to your class, home, and fellowship. They lean on you until you are uncomfortable and often infringe on your family time. You feel guilty in finally telling them you have to go, because innately you know they feel helpless without you.

The contrary response of a spiritually unbalanced Christian can be even more damaging. Once they hit what seems to be an incurable depth, they are capable of the most ungodly responses. They lash out at other Christians. They respond angrily when you set limits in your relationship. They complain to anyone within earshot about your lack of Christian compassion, and if you are a church leader, they challenge your commitment to Christ and his work.

Finally, they leave the church but never quietly. They launch a tirade that can permanently damage the reputations of those who attempted to help them. They are capable of splitting churches and upsetting God's balance in the church. They usually develop a pattern of coming to a church, joining the fellowship, thrusting themselves headlong into a variety of ministries, calling for amazing vision, encountering a problem or conflict, engaging in a public fight, and then storming out of the church in a huff. The result of their investment in that church is disturbing. Other members are injured by the shrapnel of their explosive actions. They can be hazardous to the health of a church.

Thankfully, there is hope for those who allow their emotions to guide them. The Bible shows us that even the most unstable Christian can become a productive and vital leader in the fellowship. The patron saint for the spiritually manic-depressive? The apostle Peter. God took this impetuous, often irrational man and transformed him into a productive leader in the early church. It can happen to the Harrisons of your church as well.

Peter's Journey: The Manic-Depressive Journey

Few Christians have had such a resonant and godly effect on the body of Christ as the fisherman from Galilee—Simon Peter. Andrew's brother was one of the most vocal proponents of Jesus Christ. He was also the one who betrayed our Lord in the darkest hour of his passion.

What may surprise the average Christian is that these polar opposite reactions, staunch devotion, and harsh betrayal took place in the space of just a few hours. In typical Petrine fashion, the apostle had a complete swing of emotions. He traveled from the mountaintop to the valley in less than a day.

Peter's Mountaintop: Declaration (Matt. 26:31–35)

Then Jesus said to them, "Tonight all of you will run away because of Me, for it is written: I will strike the shepherd, and the sheep of the flock will be scattered. But after I have been resurrected, I will go ahead of you to Galilee." Peter told Him, "Even if everyone runs

away because of You, I will never run away!" "I assure
you," Jesus said to him, "tonight—before the rooster
crows, you will deny Me three times!" "Even if I have
to die with You," Peter told Him, "I will never deny
You!" And all the disciples said the same thing.
(Matt. 26:31–35)

As Jesus stood on the eve of his crucifixion, his words at the
Last Supper cut through the hearts of his disciples. They had followed Jesus for over three years and had heard him speak of his
death before. At first, they thought his cryptic words were simply allegories and parables. Certainly this one they knew was
going to sit on the throne of David was not going to die. In fact,
the mother of two of the disciples even asked Jesus if they could
serve as his secretaries of state once he was inaugurated.

Jesus had other plans.

He spoke of his death, perhaps most emphatically when he
stood at the rock edifice at Caesarea Philippi, in the northeastern
corner of Israel. There, Peter had made an amazing declaration
of faith in response to Jesus' question. "'But you,' He asked them
again, 'who do you say that I am?' Peter answered Him, 'You are
the Messiah!'" (Mark 8:29).

But Jesus immediately began to speak of his death and rejection, which must have seemed odd to those who had just declared
that he would rule over all the world and overthrow any government that persecuted his children. "Then He began to teach them
that the Son of Man must suffer many things, and be rejected by
the elders, the chief priests, and the scribes, be killed, and rise
after three days" (Mark 8:31).

Peter's response to this teaching was ardent, and so too was
Jesus' response: "Peter took Him aside and began to rebuke
Him. But turning around and looking at His disciples, He
rebuked Peter and said, 'Get behind Me, Satan, because you're
not thinking about God's concerns, but man's!'" (Mark 8:32–33).

Why was Jesus calling one of his inner circle of disciples
"Satan"? His subsequent teaching seemed to indicate that even
the disciples were misunderstanding his mission. In the words of

the Messiah, to follow him was to follow him toward death. Persecution and suffering, not victory and celebration, were the markers of true devotion:

> Summoning the crowd along with His disciples, He said to them, "If anyone wants to be My follower, he must deny himself, take up his cross, and follow Me. For whoever wants to save his life will lose it, but whoever loses his life because of Me and the gospel will save it. For what does it benefit a man to gain the whole world yet lose his life? What can a man give in exchange for his life? For whoever is ashamed of Me and of My words in this adulterous and sinful generation, the Son of Man will also be ashamed of him when He comes in the glory of His Father with the holy angels." (Mark 8:34–38)

It was a declaration that none of the disciples, much less Peter, quite understood. As they lounged at the table that would be their last gathering, Jesus spoke in terms that were not just intimate to his experience (crucifixion) but to theirs as well (betrayal). He told them that they, too would desert him in his final hours.

Peter's declaration of fidelity in Matthew 26 was echoed by the other disciples as well. But to Peter specifically, Jesus spoke words that must have pierced his heart. "Not only are you going to leave Me," Jesus said, "but you will deny any knowledge of Me three times." It must have deflated any hopes of a heroic stance by this emotional disciple.

Peter's Valley: Dozing and Denial (Matt. 26:36–75)

The next events, so significant in our redemption, happened within the space of one day. Jesus was betrayed by Judas, captured by the authorities, tried in three separate trials before Annas, Caiaphas, and Pilate, and was crucified. Yet from our perspective, few made such a schizophrenic journey as Peter. In this short span of time, Peter went from taking up arms to defend Jesus to weeping bitterly.

We first find Peter asleep during Christ's darkest hour. This brought a rebuke from the Lord which must have cut Peter to the bone. Jesus seemed to diagnose Peter's predicament when he noted that the "spirit is willing, but the flesh is weak" (Matt. 26:41). Peter, could you not stay awake a single hour for the one you said you would never betray?

Then, immediately following Peter's slumber during Christ's prayer of agony in the garden, Judas arrived with the mob. This gathering of Jewish elders, chief priests, and armed soldiers arrested Jesus after Judas identified him with a kiss of disloyalty. Surely the other disciples were frozen with fear, but not Peter. This impetuous follower of Christ impulsively unsheathed his sword. The resulting action brought about a rebuke by Jesus:

At that moment one of those with Jesus reached out his hand and drew his sword. He struck the high priest's slave and cut off his ear. Then Jesus told him, "Put your sword back in place because all who take up a sword will perish by a sword. Or do you think that I cannot call on My Father, and He will provide Me at once with more than 12 legions of angels? How, then, would the Scriptures be fulfilled that say it must happen this way?" (Matt. 26:51–54)

Peter must have been confused and hurt. Here he took decisive action to defend his Lord, and instead of commendation he received a scolding! One must wonder what the other disciples were thinking. Though Matthew does not tell us Peter's name, John does (John 18:10), and Luke even notes that Jesus healed Malchus's ear (Luke 22:51). Matthew 26:56 ends with these ominous words: "Then all the disciples deserted Him and ran away."

In the ensuing trials, the focus of Scripture is firmly upon our Savior, as he was abandoned and accused by the authorities and religious leaders. Still, Peter is woven throughout the narrative. He is always seen as one who cannot bring himself to completely leave the scene but seems torn between survival and devotion. When Jesus was brought before Caiaphas, Matthew tells us, "Peter was following Him at a distance right to the high priest's courtyard. He went in and was sitting with the temple police to see the outcome" (Matt. 26:58).

Of course, the next phase in Peter's renunciation of Christ is equally notorious. A servant spotted him in the courtyard and identified him as a disciple. John's Gospel tells us that Peter was standing near the fire that the police and slaves had built to ward off the cold night air. Peter replied to their inquiry, "I don't know what you're talking about" (Matt. 26:70).

As Peter attempted to blend into the crowd outside of Caiaphas's home, a woman recognized him, and this time, Matthew tells us he swore that he did not know the man ("with an oath," Matt. 26:72). Interestingly, one would think that after such a close call, Peter would scurry away and be thankful he was not arrested. Yet John tells us that he lingered in the same place.

One can see the anguish with which Peter was dealing. His first denial was a feigned attempt at bewilderment, as if to say, "This woman is crazy! I do not have a clue what she is talking about!" He did not actually deny Jesus. He simply pretended to be puzzled by her words. At the second identification, though, Peter not only denied his connection with Jesus but also sealed it by swearing an oath (Matt. 26:69–72).

His final betrayal of Jesus, however, left no room for doubt. Peter must have felt that he had fooled the crowd. One of Malchus's relatives spotted him and remembered him from his garden swordplay (John 18:26). Others noticed that he had the distinct accent of a northerner from Galilee (Matt. 26:73). As Peter felt the walls closing in around him, he spoke with the forcefulness of one of Christ's strongest antagonists. Matthew tells us: "Then he started to curse and to swear with an oath, 'I do not know the man!'" (Matt. 26:74).

At this third and final disavowal, Jesus' prophecy comes true. "Immediately, a rooster crowed, and Peter remembered the words Jesus had spoken . . . and he went outside and wept bitterly" (Matt. 26:74–75). Luke's Gospel adds an even more grievous detail that the other three Gospels do not. Luke tells us that Jesus

was near Peter when this third betrayal took place, and he turned
and looked at Peter at that precise moment (Luke 22:61).

Peter had gone from being Jesus' strongest defender to
being his most adamant adversary in just one night.

Symptoms of a Spiritually Manic-Depressive Saint

Peter's journey from the height of emotions to the depths of
depression, sadly, is not a solitary experience. Many Christians
have the same affliction. They are unstable emotionally. Perhaps
the most shocking element of their travail is that they themselves
do not recognize their affliction. Like Simon Peter, they are just
reacting and responding to circumstances and crises. As with
Luke's addition to the story of Peter's betrayal, it takes Jesus to
get them to recognize the profound gravity of their disease.

Yet their effects upon a church can be devastating. The damage a manic-depressive can have on an individual church can be
almost irreparable. The Christian leaders who learn to recognize
the symptoms of a person infected with this spiritual malady can
not only prevent the problems they can cause but can also help
those persons resolve the issues that beleaguer them.

A Spiritually Unstable Person Is Impulsive

Impulsiveness is the driving response mechanism for the
unstable Christian. He acts before he thinks, and he assumes that
he is prepared for virtually anything. This is the exact opposite of
a careful and meditative person who proceeds with caution and
forethought.

The Bible is full of teachings concerning our response mech-
anisms in crisis. Ecclesiastes 5:2 even tells us to avoid impulsiveness before God himself: "Do not be hasty to speak, and do not
be impulsive to make a speech before God. God is in heaven and
you are on earth, so let your words be few."

Spiritual caution is a call from God to avoid impetuousness.
If we consider the implications of our actions, often we avoid
jumping into things that we will regret later. Notice that at the

outset of God's commands to the Israelites he repeated the phrase "be careful," to specifically call them to forethought and right action:

> Be careful to do as the LORD your God has commanded you; you are not to turn aside to the right or the left. (Deut. 5:32)

> Listen, Israel, and be careful to follow [them], so that you may prosper and multiply greatly, because the LORD, the God of your fathers, has promised you a land flowing with milk and honey. (Deut. 6:3)

> Be careful not to forget the LORD who brought you out of the land of Egypt, out of the place of slavery. (Deut. 6:12)

> Righteousness will be ours if we are careful to follow every one of these commands before the LORD our God, as He has commanded us. (Deut. 6:25)

> If you listen to and are careful to keep these ordinances, the LORD your God will keep His covenant loyalty with you, as He swore to your fathers. (Deut. 7:12)

David understood the importance of thoughtful action. His dying admonition to his son Solomon, who would become the next king of Israel, included these ominous words: "And so that the LORD will carry out His promise that He made to me: 'If your sons are careful to walk faithfully before Me with their whole mind and heart, you will never fail to have a man on the throne of Israel'" (1 Kings 2:4). Surely King Solomon would have wished that he and his sons would have followed David's warning. Israel would not have been split in half had they not acted impetuously.

Indeed, as Jehu's reign was evaluated in 2 Kings, we find him as one afflicted with the impulsiveness we later see in Peter: "Yet, Jehu was not careful to follow with all his heart the law of the LORD God of Israel. He did not turn from the sins that Jeroboam had caused Israel to commit" (2 Kings 10:31).

The New Testament also contains great insights into the judicious and prudent actions and beliefs of the strong Christian and the strong church:

Be careful not to practice your righteousness in front of people, to be seen by them. Otherwise, you will have no reward from your Father in heaven. (Matt. 6:1)

According to God's grace that was given to me, as a skilled master builder I have laid a foundation, and another builds on it. But each one must be careful how he builds on it. (1 Cor. 3:10)

But be careful that this right of yours in no way becomes a stumbling block to the weak. (1 Cor. 8:9)

Therefore, whoever thinks he stands must be careful not to fall! (1 Cor. 10:12)

Pay careful attention, then, to how you walk—not as unwise people but as wise. (Eph. 5:15)

Be careful that no one takes you captive through philosophy and empty deceit based on human tradition, based on the elemental forces of the world, and not based on Christ. (Col. 2:8)

This saying is trustworthy. I want you to insist on these things, so that those who have believed God might be careful to devote themselves to good works. These are good and profitable for everyone. (Titus 3:8)

Notice the emphasis on the actions of the church body, especially in Paul's words to the Corinthian church. Could it be that this ragged fellowship suffered great problems precisely because they were impetuous?

Do not confuse caution with inactivity. Cautious Christians always act, but they act on wisdom and prayer rather than emotion and feeling. The Christian who is always jumping to action often jumps ahead of God! This can lead to unresolved problems, unfulfilled dreams and plans, and an unhealthy Christian walk. Like Peter, the unstable Christian is always having to apologize and "eat his words."

A Spiritually Unstable Person Lives by Feelings and Emotion

Nothing is more tragic than a Christian who measures his Christianity by emotional standards. Nothing is more catastrophic than a church that grows solely due to emotions and feelings. Both are more prevalent than we are willing to admit.

If you do not believe such scenarios take place, consider this example. A church that is averaging two hundred in attendance calls a new pastor and a new worship leader. Both are charismatic men with personalities that drip with enthusiasm. Both have the capacity to excite the church and draw them closer to God. The worship leader puts together a worship experience that is exhilarating. The pastor preaches with passion and conviction.

Does the church grow? Of course it does.

Yet what if the pastor does not really feed the people the Word of God but preaches sermons filled with clichés and positive thinking? What if he uses illustrations that cause people to weep and laugh, even though they may not be biblical? What if the worship pastor leads each worship service to a crescendo of emotion and feeling? Do you think the church will continue to grow?

Of course it will. Sadly, this is often the picture of the modern church. It is a mile wide—and about an inch deep.

Yet the downside of such a church, built upon feeling and emotion, is the same for a church body as it is for the individual believer. As soon as the feeling diminishes, as soon as the excitement lessens, the church dies. When a new church opens up that offers a more profound feeling and a deeper experience, then the people leave the first church and join the next one.

It does not happen overnight. First, the people begin to lament the lack of joy in the first church. They begin to murmur about the "loss of the Holy Spirit's power" in the first church. The reduction of sensation—often seen in tears, shouting, and passion—is bemoaned as a loss of God's very presence. The people begin to search for a new place that equals the emotional plateaus to which they were drawn initially. The leaders of the church learn the sad truth, often ignored: What it takes to get them there, it will take to keep them there.

For individual Christians, such a search is also devastating. When the emotional levels begin to lessen, they begin to blame themselves. Since they are driven by emotions, the loss of emotional fervor must mean a loss of spiritual power. Since they cannot blame the church, they begin to blame themselves. They begin to accuse themselves of backsliding, as if they do not love Jesus as much as they used to.

This begins a vicious cycle.

We are not being critical of emotional worship. In fact, we are both very passionate preachers. However, when emotion rather than faith and confidence in God is given the reins of the heart, this spiritual crash is inevitable. To use the classic formulation, every Christian and every church needs *logos* (the Word), *pathos* (passion), and *ethos* (application and obedience). Of the three, only the Word is perfect. Experiences can be deceptive, and feelings fade. Only the Bible is trustworthy.

Think of it this way: The emotions you experienced on the day of your wedding diminish, don't they? That epiphany of tears and joy as you declared your undying love for each other rarely can be matched. Now, move ahead three years. You have gotten used to each other. You have fought over inconsequential issues on occasion. You have seen what the other person looks like, first thing in the morning.

The feelings do fade a bit. Does that mean you are no longer in love? Of course not. Love is a commitment and a covenant, not a feeling. It is the same with your walk with God. Commitment to God is not measured by the way you feel; it is measured by your devotion.

A Spiritually Unstable Christian Dwells on Experiences, Not Faith

Since certain experiences provoke certain feelings, the unstable Christian, like Peter, begins to seek ways to duplicate that experience. Did you experience a "high" while at church camp? Then you will seek to duplicate the church camp feelings. You volunteer for activities and events with the desire to reproduce the same feeling and experience.

When you copy the behavior and imitate the actions you remember, but do not produce the same feeling, the unstable Christian immediately becomes permeated with doubt. The event was the same. The actions were the same. The feeling was not the same. Someone must be to blame.

Some unstable Christians begin to doubt themselves. Like our illustrative Harrison, they begin to question their salvation or devotion to God. They wonder if their commitment was genuine, since they are measuring their salvation by their emotion. They hear testimonies of radical conversions where the convert was ablaze with glory, and they begin to wonder, *Was my salvation real? I didn't feel like that!* Yet salvation is based on faith, not feeling (Eph. 2:8). It is a commitment rather than an emotion.

Some unstable Christians begin to doubt their church. They are notorious for causing fights in the fellowship, starting confrontations because they no longer see any evidence of the "power of God." The evidence they seek is emotional in scope. Without the feeling, they deduce, there is no power. The truly unstable Christian, when confronted with a less emotional church, eventually stops coming to church altogether! If he cannot match the initial "tingly feeling" he once experienced, then he sees all attempts at finding another match for that feeling as futile.

If I can't get that excitement back, I don't want to go anywhere.

Sadly, that is a chorus sung by more people than we care to admit.

Still, there is hope. Peter discovered the God of the second chance and the God of restoration.

Peter's Fate and God's Faithfulness (John 21:1–25)

If we were truly honest, most of us would have written Peter off after his third denial of Christ. After all, was not his crime equal to that of Judas? Both had denied Christ, and both were publicly censured. Judas's betrayal took place in the garden. Peter's took place in the alleyway. Yet both were treasonous.

The Gospel of Matthew never mentions Peter again, after his betrayal.

Mark just mentions him once, and it is interesting what he chooses to include. When Mary Magdalene, Mary the mother of James, and Salome approached the tomb and discovered it empty, they found an angel inside. The stone had been rolled away, and Jesus was alive. Mark quotes the angel with these words: "'Don't be alarmed,' he told them. 'You are looking for Jesus the Nazarene, who was crucified. He has been resurrected! He is not here! See the place where they put Him. But go, tell His disciples *and Peter*, "He is going ahead of you to Galilee; you will see Him there just as He told you"'" (Mark 16:6–7).

Read that again. Why did the angel single out Peter? Was he not hiding in the same place as the rest of the men, or was he no longer considered one of the disciples? Luke 24:9 notes that the women returned to town and found the eleven remaining disciples together, so these are not plausible options.

Was Peter's crime and sin unforgivable? Did it make him unqualified as a servant of God? For some churches and Christians, the answer would be a resounding *yes*. In their theology and practice, Peter was now disqualified for service, having publicly disavowed Christ in his darkest hour. To some, Peter was now a reprobate. Even Luke mentions Peter only once more, showing him running to the tomb after the women reported it empty and returning back amazed (Luke 24:12).

The apostle John, however, tells us the story of Peter's restoration. In John 20:1–10, Peter and John race to the tomb together and discover that Jesus had in fact been resurrected. When Jesus appeared to Mary Magdalene and she ran and exclaimed, "I have seen the Lord," the disciples rejoiced that Christ had conquered death (John 20:11–18).

When Jesus finally appeared to the disciples and said, "Peace to you," they were filled with joy and hope. The emphasis of the story is not on Peter but Thomas, who was not present in the room where the disciples had been hiding. The Bible tells us that the ten disciples tried to convince Thomas that they had seen the Lord, but to no avail. He did not believe until Christ told him to touch his nail scars. Then Thomas exclaimed, "My Lord and my God!" (John 20:24–29).

Still, it must have been awkward for Peter. All the other disciples were aware of his denial of Christ. Many had even witnessed his sedition. How did he live among them during those days? Did he offer excuses? Did he sit quietly to the side, rejected by the rest of them? We will never know.

What we do know, however, is that Jesus himself did not reject Peter. After a period of time, Peter, Thomas, Nathanael, the brothers James and John, and two other disciples decided to go fishing under the cover of darkness. They had hidden in a locked room out of fear for almost two weeks, and now Peter led them to the Sea of Galilee. They had left Jerusalem and headed home, back to their old vocations. After an entire night of fishing, they had caught nothing (John 21:1–3).

At daybreak, Jesus appeared on the shore. The seven disciples did not recognize him at first, but when he told them to cast their nets on the right side of the boat, and they caught so many fish they could not lift the nets into the boats, John said to Peter, "It is the Lord!" (John 21:4–7).

Peter immediately put on his robe and (once again) impetuously jumped into the water, swimming the one hundred yards to shore. The disciples saw a charcoal fire and fish already prepared. Jesus told them to bring their fish—all 153 of them—to him, and he invited them to have breakfast with him (John 21:4–13).

After breakfast, Jesus turned his attention to the fallen Peter. Two times, Jesus asked him the same question:

"Simon, son of John, do you love Me more than these?" "Yes, Lord," he said to Him, "You know that I love You." "Feed My lambs," He told him. (John 21:15)

A second time He asked him, "Simon, son of John, do you love Me?" "Yes, Lord," he said to Him, "You know that I love You." "Shepherd My sheep," He told him. (John 21:16)

Surely, Peter was thinking exactly what the other disciples were thinking. Jesus' questions were cutting to his heart. Could he really state that he loved Jesus when he had so loudly denied him three times? Peter must have thought that Jesus was punishing him for his sins.

> The final question, however, exposed Peter's pain over his sin: He asked him the third time, "Simon, son of John, do you love Me?" Peter was grieved that He asked him the third time, "Do you love Me?" He said, "Lord, You know everything! You know that I love You." "Feed My sheep," Jesus said. "I assure you: When you were young, you would tie your belt and walk wherever you wanted. But when you grow old, you will stretch out your hands and someone else will tie you and carry you where you don't want to go." He said this to signify by what kind of death he would glorify God. After saying this, He told him, "Follow Me!" (John 21:17–19)

Jesus had not given up on Peter. Three times Peter had denied Jesus, and now three times Peter confessed his love for Jesus. In each instance, Jesus called Peter to confirm his love for Christ by serving the children of God. In fact, Jesus noted that Peter's love would be tested again, when he would follow Christ to his own martyrdom. Jesus told Peter that his own death would glorify God as well.

Before we miss the point of Jesus' restoration of Peter and assume that death is the only way to restore a fallen brother, John tells us:

> Peter turned around and saw the disciple Jesus loved following them. . . . When Peter saw him, he said to Jesus, "Lord—what about him?" "If I want him to remain until I come," Jesus answered, "what is that to you? As for you, follow Me." So this report spread to the brothers that this disciple would not die. Yet Jesus did not tell him that he would not die, but, "If I want

him to remain until I come, what is that to you?"
(John 21:20–23)

The point of the story was that Peter, the impulsive, impetuous, emotional, often unstable disciple of Christ, was restored by
Christ. Jesus made Peter usable by transforming him into a
mature believer. As the early church grew in the book of Acts,
that maturity would become necessary, as thousands came to
faith in Christ, and as persecution arose in the land.

And before you write off the impetuous and impulsive and
unstable members of your church, please ask yourself these
questions:

- Who did God call on to preach the inaugural sermon of
  the church? (Acts 2:14–36).
- Who boldly proclaimed Jesus as the Messiah before the
  very group to whom he disavowed any knowledge of
  Jesus just weeks before? (Acts 4:5–21).
- Who told the inquirers to "repent and be baptized in the
  name of Jesus the Messiah"? (Acts 2:38).

It was that formerly manic-depressive, impulsive, and unstable apostle Peter. God can restore anyone willing to turn everything—even their emotions—over to him. God did not lessen
Peter's passion or fervor; he *harnessed* them for his glory.

Chapter 9

The Martha Syndrome: Obsessive-Compulsive Christians

Manic Ministrie and Misguided Micromanagers
Luke 22:24–30

Ruby never said no. Ever.

Before you think that we are discussing a woman of questionable morals, we ask you to reconsider.

This is not the story of an immoral woman.

This is the story of a kinetic woman, and her disease is equally lethal. As a matter of fact, her condition is widespread; you will immediately identify your own particular "Ruby."

Ruby was a faithful and humble Christian in one of our early churches. She prayed daily and even kept a prayer journal. She read her Bible regularly, which was heavily marked up with years of notes from sermons she had heard and lessons she had taught. She rarely missed a service, though she was perpetually late to every service, meeting, and session at church. But she always had a reason.

You see, Ruby was always in motion. She was the most faithful member of the church, and it was slowly killing her.

If ever there was an overworked Christian, it was Ruby. She taught the fourth-grade Bible study class every Sunday. She had been teaching the class for so long that she even had a college student assistant in the class whom she had taught fifteen years before.

Ruby served on six standing committees: the finance committee, building and grounds committee, youth committee, and women's ministry committee. She was the chairperson of the personnel committee and the historical committee. Virtually every Sunday afternoon, Ruby could be found in some classroom, sitting around a table discussing some aspect of ministry in the church, drinking bad coffee from a small Styrofoam cup.

She had even developed the habit of not going home on Sunday afternoons. After everyone would make their way to the parking lot after the morning service, Ruby would begin to straighten up her classroom, putting away the crayons and craft materials. Then, after her various committee meetings, she would study the materials for the Discipleship Training class she was taking. Since she was usually three or four days behind, she used the time to catch up. Secretly, she would mark something on every page, even though she just scanned the lesson and work. She hated to look like she did not do the work. Thus, each page included random notations she had made. Other women marveled at her ability to juggle so many ministries, but only Ruby knew her secret: she was always days behind and tired, and she usually did just enough to look like she was keeping up.

Her schedule through the week was no better.

On Monday mornings, she attended the weekly woman's Bible study. Since she did not actually teach the lesson, she often volunteered to bake muffins, or write notes to new visitors, or call those who had missed a number of classes.

On Tuesday afternoons, Ruby served in the church clothes closet, where impoverished families would come and get clothing and supplies. After she helped there, she would often pack grocery sacks for the food pantry for the poor, even though she was not actually signed up for the work.

Wednesdays were as busy as Sundays for Ruby. Beginning precisely at 1:00 PM, Ruby began working in the kitchen, helping with the Wednesday night fellowship supper team. For four hours, these ladies (and some men) would prepare food for over three hundred people. The rationale for the fellowship meal was that it allowed busy people who worked to come straight from the office to the church, get a meal at a cheap price, and then attend the evening studies.

The interesting thing is, virtually every Wednesday after the meal, Ruby would seethe internally. As she would quickly put on the uniform for her missions and discipleship program for the kids, she would see members of the church who would leisurely linger at the tables in the fellowship hall. She knew they did not go upstairs to the pastor's Wednesday night class. She *knew* it. After an hour or so, they would slip out and go home, and it infuriated her. How dare they come and be blessed by the meal but not come to the classes?

Thursdays, Fridays, and Saturdays were no different for Ruby. She regularly went out on visitation. She attended "cottage prayer meetings." She would chaperone countless youth events and trips. She even cleaned the church during those periods where she felt the church was looking a little dirty or messy. In any given week, Ruby was in the church, serving in some capacity, five or six days.

Are you tired yet?

We got tired just typing this!

Welcome to Ruby's world. Every pastor, every associate pastor, and every ministry leader knew they could count on Ruby. She never saw a need she did not fill, and she never saw a committee on which she did not serve. Ruby was the Lord's "superwoman." The whole church knew it. The mantra went: "When in need call Ruby."

Even her family had adjusted to Ruby's schedule of church work. Her husband even wondered what to do when she was home. Her children often accompanied their mother to the church to help out, but gradually they developed lives of their own. Home, for Ruby, her husband, and the children, was a place to change clothes, eat quick meals, and sleep. It was more like an office than a home.

On the surface, one would assume that Ruby was simply a committed Christian. Sadly, this was not the case. Ruby was afflicted. She was afflicted with "Martha Syndrome," an obsessive compulsiveness that drove her to work incessantly in the church. She was a boiling cauldron of insecurity and resentment. Ruby—indeed all "Rubys"—needed help.

The Patron Saint of Ministry Mania: Martha of Bethany

Jesus had few friends who were as close to him as a family in Bethany. Three siblings, Lazarus, Martha, and Mary, served as an adopted family to Christ. Living in Bethany, just a few miles east of Jerusalem, Lazarus and his sisters gave Jesus refuge from the throngs of crowds that followed him in his public ministry. Mentioned twelve times in the New Testament, this trio was so close to our Lord that John 11:5 notes, "Jesus loved Martha, her sister, and Lazarus." He wept at Lazarus's unexpected death, even though he would resurrect him later (John 11:35). If Jesus ever had a place to relax during his years on the earth, it was the Bethany home of Lazarus, Martha, and Mary.

But in the various narratives of the family, one begins to spot a pattern, especially germane to our discussion. Whenever one finds Martha in the story, she is obsessed with time and consumed by work. She is always rushing about, as if to press others into her time schedule. Notice:

1. In John 11, when Lazarus dies, Jesus is summoned to their home, two miles from Jerusalem. When Martha gets word that Jesus is approaching, she leaves Mary at home to rush to

meet him on the road (John 11:20). John even gives the detail that she had run to meet Christ outside the village (John 11:30).

2. Amazingly, she offers Christ a rebuke: "Lord," Martha said to Jesus, "if you had been here, my brother wouldn't have died" (John 11:21).

3. Jesus responded by promising a miracle. As astounding as this moment must have been, Martha interjected at Jesus' words with her own time-obsessed statement: "Lord," said Martha, the sister of the dead man, "he already stinks. It's been four days." (John 11:39).

Do you see a common thread in Martha's words? She is obsessed with timely action. For Martha, it seems that delay is the worst offense. Schedules must be kept, and deadlines lost are the most egregious sins. Does it seem to you that Martha could have easily said, "Lord, if you had only followed my timetable, all of this could have been prevented?"

The second component of the "Martha Syndrome" is equally as insidious. Martha is a perpetually moving, continuously serving, exhaustingly volunteering saint of God! One gets tired just *watching* her. Take as an example the celebration following Lazarus's resurrection. One finds an interesting combination of positions among the siblings:

Six days before the Passover, Jesus came to Bethany where Lazarus was, the one Jesus had raised from the dead. So they gave a dinner for Him there; Martha was serving them, and Lazarus was one of those reclining at the table with Him. Then Mary took a pound of fragrant oil—pure and expensive nard—anointed Jesus' feet, and wiped His feet with her hair. So the house was filled with the fragrance of the oil. (John 12:1–3)

Though we often focus on the confrontation between Judas's money obsession and Mary's love offering, the neglected feature is the positions of the three hosts: Lazarus is reclining at the table, near the one who brought him to life again. Mary is worshipping Christ at his feet. But where is Martha? John 12:2 tells us—Martha is serving the guests.

Martha's response at the miracles and movement of Christ in their midst is to get busy! Kinetic movement, rather than worshipful adoration, is her first impulse.

OCD Christianity: The Symptoms of Martha

Until this point, the "Marthas" and "Rubys" of this world have some justification for their actions. After all, where would our churches be? Their rationalization can be simply outlined:

- The Lord's work never gets done.
- Someone has to take care of the details.
- Not everyone needs the spotlight; people are needed behind the scenes.
- If I don't do it, it never gets done.
- If I want to do these things, what is wrong with that?

Yet Jesus intercedes on our behalf in this study. In Luke's only mention of the family in Bethany, Jesus' words to Martha detail his response to those who feel their service is indispensable to the Lord. In Luke 10, Jesus is found at the Lazarus home, in the midst of a rest stop where Martha has little rest:

While they were traveling, He entered a village, and a woman named Martha welcomed Him into her home. She had a sister named Mary, who also sat at the Lord's feet and was listening to what He said. But Martha was distracted by her many tasks, and she came up and asked, "Lord, don't You care that my sister has left me to serve alone? So tell her to give me a hand." (Luke 10:38–40)

On the surface, one would guess that Mary is the culpable suspect of the story. Here is Martha, with unexpected guests in their home, trying to ensure that everyone is comfortable. She is serving the Lord and serving the people, and she finds her sister lounging about and doing nothing. Surely Martha is justified in asking the Lord to rebuke Mary for her perceived laziness. Right?

Wrong.

Luke hints at Martha's condition in Luke 10:40: "Martha was distracted by her many tasks." The fundamental truth in this situation cannot be overemphasized: *Martha was distracted by that* *which was important, but neglected that which was essential.*

To Martha, Jesus responded gently but firmly: "Martha, Martha, you are worried and upset about many things, but one thing is necessary. Mary has made the right choice, and it will not be taken away from her" (Luke 10:41–42).

A painful reprimand, but worthy of investigation. An OCD Christian compulsively obsesses on those distractions that consume our time, but also rob us of the joy of the Christian life. Service is helpful, and serving God in various ministries can be a wonderful blessing. But a Christian who goes overboard in service is in danger of losing any benefits of service, because the service itself becomes a sin. It becomes the end instead of the means.

Diagnosis: The Symptoms of the Martha Syndrome

More than likely you know many "Marthas." The more difficult question could be, Are you infected with the Martha Syndrome? Since self-diagnosis and self-evaluation are rare gifts, we have developed a number of benchmarks that will help you. If you answer any number of these questions in the affirmative, then perhaps you have become an unwitting carrier of the Martha Syndrome.

The Test of Multiple Ministries

Be honest. Into how many ministries are you invested? Is your home time and personal spiritual time sapped by the number of times you have to go to the church? A person afflicted with the Martha Syndrome does not easily notice the sheer breadth of his service, because he has become accustomed to his hectic schedules. Ask yourself this question: Am I spending more time at the church than other members who are also faithful?

The Test of the Volunteer

A true "Martha" does not have the capacity to say no. You are approached by a church member with a great idea or wonderful opportunity, and your first impulse is to say no. You genuinely want to say no. But you find yourself eventually saying yes. Why?

You begin to envision this ministry failing miserably. You picture this person disappointed. Secretly, you know, beyond the shadow of a doubt, that if you are involved in the event, it will succeed. Thus, you slowly acquiesce. You begin to juggle your schedule in your mind, finding ways to balance your already-heavy schedule with one more event. You are tireless in your service — and exhausted.

The Test of Delegation

Sadly, this is one of the most telling symptoms of the OCD saint. Can you delegate? Let us put it another way that might be a bit clearer: Do you assign people to help in your work, but inevitably you do the actual work yourself? This is a sign of a driven perfectionist, but it also bespeaks a deeper spiritual problem. On some level, you simply do not trust others to get the job done the way you would do it. Does this resonate with you? If you would be genuinely honest, would you admit that you are silently critical of other ministries? Do you watch other church activities unfold and think that it would have been a success *if only* you had been the leader? This is symptomatic of a deep underlying misunderstanding of the body of Christ: You feel indispensable to the Lord.

The Test of Guilty Rest

Ask yourself these questions: Do you begin to feel "itchy" if you sit still and relax for a period of time? Do you begin to make mental lists silently, so that you are not exactly resting but actually just planning? Do you feel guilty when you have nothing to do? Whether you like it or not, you are probably a Martha. She could not simply enjoy the presence of Christ in her home;

she had to be *doing* something. She served tables. She prepared food. She could not justify resting before the Lord. Unfortunately, she has many children in the Lord's work today.

We often joke to one another that this is a *pastoral poison.* Many pastors are infected with this ailment, and they know it. Someday we hope to write a book for pastors about the predicament of modern pastoring. It would be called *I Never Had a Sabbath!*

Think about it: The day of rest, Sunday, was established in the New Testament as a sign of our covenant with the risen Lord. It was the equivalent of the Jewish Sabbath (Saturday) that was a purposeful day of inactivity. Yet it is precisely this day that is the busiest for the ministers of God.

We arrive early, set everything up, and some even teach a Bible study class. Then, while the members are seated, we stand and preach passionately. Following the service, we shake hands, counsel, and meet with people. We may rush home for a quick lunch, but inevitably we rush to the church in the afternoon for meetings. Then, we do it all over again for the evening service. By the time we get home late that evening, the entire day—this day established for the rest in God—is a blur. Is this true rest?

The Test of Secret Resentment

Perhaps the most difficult test of the Martha Syndrome is one that only you can answer. A true "Martha" innately feels unappreciated.

Please remember, a Martha-type Christian is not a weak Christian. Indeed, when Jesus asked Martha if she believed her dead brother could live, she rightly responded that Lazarus would resurrect in the last day (John 11:24). She also clearly proclaimed Christ's divinity by referring to him as "Lord" (John 11:27). A "Martha" knows Christ and his Word without question.

A "Martha," though, may love the Lord, but she feels inherently unloved by the people of God. She knows her service is exemplary. Why doesn't the pastor and church recognize that fact?

She also feels misunderstood. If she ever voices a complaint about her exhaustion, she feels that those to whom she is speaking cannot truly comprehend the depth of her sacrifice. After all, they aren't serving Christ like she is.

The irony is, even though a "Martha" may complain, she really doesn't know any other way to serve God. More than likely, she served like this, even before her salvation, in other contexts. A "Martha" type of person is a professional volunteer. School functions, car pools, charity events, and a myriad of other organizations benefit from the labor of a "Martha." The only one who does not benefit from her labor is "Martha" herself.

Prognosis: Curing the OCD Christian

Obviously, an obsessive workaholic Christian needs help. Interestingly, this is the one lethal poison out of the litany that is not highly contagious. Instead, it is a disease that kills the carrier. Tragically, those who are infected with the Martha Syndrome are the hardest workers you know. Do you see the severity of this disease? It kills those who are your closest members and friends.

The progression of the disease is clear. Some "Marthas" just have a type of breakdown. Suddenly, shockingly, they quit. Additionally, they do not quit one or two ministries, for this would involve evaluating the importance of the various works in which she is invested. Since they are all equally vital to a "Martha," she cannot make such a decision. Instead, she makes a clean break from everything and enters the realm of the "former servants of God." The rationale goes, "If I cannot serve in all of them, then I will not serve in any of them."

In the days that follow her mass resignations, most Martha-types watch closely to see if she is missed. Often, a Martha-type can be talked back into service by showing her that the work dis-integrates without her. We would vigorously disagree with this approach, however, because it plays into her worst fears. The "Martha" has her belief that she is indispensable reinforced. Since we are told that the hardest workers in the average church last only seven years, reenlisting a "Martha" only quickens her untimely demise.

In fact, we believe a bit of pastoral intervention is the ultimate cure here. If the pastor and the church forcibly limit the number of ministries in which members can work, then they are lengthening the lives of countless "Marthas," who are then given an irrefutable *no*, since it is a church policy, not her choice. Some ministries may suffer in the short term after the implementation of such a policy, but the church will be strengthened in the long run. Members who are not quickly burning out are usually better Christians. Certainly they are happier!

Second, the "Marthas" in our churches need to make a profound discovery: They are not indispensable to God! They are precious souls and godly people, but the Lord's work continued for years before they came around. Instead, the inversion of the principle is the central principle. A walk with God—a true, abiding, and joyous walk with God—is indispensable to our service.

Third, one must admit that being an OCD Christian is a true misunderstanding of the grace of God. Many serve in this capacity because they feel that "the more I do for God, the more he will love me." The guilt they feel in saying no is directed not at the person, but ultimately it is directed at God. They feel that if they say no, they are rejecting God. This is a tragic misunderstanding. God gives the talents, and we must use them, but it is better to do a few things well than many things poorly.

Finally, there is a fundamental theological question we must ask rhetorically.

- Why did God rest on the seventh day after creation?
- Was he tired after creating all the universe and humanity in six days?
- Was the sheer daunting task of creation so draining to God that he needed a break?

Of course, the answer is no. Genesis 2:2–3 says, "By the seventh day, God completed His work that He had done, and He rested on the seventh day from all His work that He had done. God blessed the seventh day and declared it holy, for on it He rested from His work of creation."

God did not need the rest. God blessed the Sabbath rest. He did so for our benefit, not his. We are commanded to rest.

Do you think God knows better than we do?

In many new cars that have navigation systems and built-in compasses, if you are not careful you can turn them off. One young lady with a new car was driving in the rain and turned on what she thought were the windshield wipers. However, the wipers did not come on but across the dashboard came the message, "Drive car in 360 degrees." She had no idea what that meant. When she arrived home she went straight to the car manual to find what the message could possibly be.

She learned that while trying to turn on the wipers she had turned off the internal compass. The car in a sense lost its sense of direction. To correct the problem you have to reset the internal compass by driving the car in a full circle and pointing it north. This resets the system.

For so many people who live their lives in an obsessive and compulsive manner, filled with so much activity that it drains the joy out of living, they need to stop. Then they should get pointed in the direction of Christ and allow his Holy Spirit to reset their spiritual system. That is what worship is all about. That is why the Lord says in Psalm 46:10, "Stop [your fighting]—and know that I am God." The word literally means "stop fighting with your internal drives." Some translate it to mean "lay down your arms in a type of surrender." When our lives are so obsessive and full of compulsive behaviors that they are wearying and frustrating, we need to surrender all our activities to God and reflect on the fact that he is God and we are not. We need our internal spiritual compass reset by the only one capable of doing it—Jesus Christ.

Chapter 10

Phobias: The Fearful and the Faithful

Timothy and the Church at Ephesus
2 Timothy 1:3–7

If Julie could have strangled her husband, she would have.

But strangling a pastor was a crime.

If she had reminded him once, she had reminded him a hundred times about Charlie, but her husband never seemed to listen. She assumed it was just his selective memory. After all, how could a man who had memorized entire sections of Spurgeon's sermons not remember that Charlie never wanted to be called on to pray?

And yet, there they stood in the service, before God and man, and her husband had called on Charlie to pray before the offering. The silence was deafening.

In the five years that Stanley had been pastor of the suburban Raleigh, North Carolina, church, the congregation had seen tremendous growth, from about fifty in attendance when he came to more than three hundred. Many had attributed the growth to Brother Stanley's effervescent personality. He exuded joy and confidence but was a humble man as well. He was the type of pastor who never answered when someone called him "Doctor," though he had indeed earned his doctorate.

His sermons pulsed with energy, and the staff he worked with was also exciting. The youth department and music programs were wonderful, and along with his sermons, served as a beacon to a community that responded by attending the church in droves. The church had added a second service and stood on the precipice of adding another, while the long-range planning committee studied a plan to build a new sanctuary.

Yet the secret to the church's growth was actually no secret at all. Stan, as he liked to be called, built a team of laymen around him who were active, faithful, and loyal. Wives who had seen their husbands rise to leadership after years of inertia just smiled every Sunday as they saw their husbands serve as greeters, workers, teachers, and ushers. This squadron of thirty men served as the backbone of the church, and the church ran like a well-oiled machine because of it. Rarely was there a need or problem that these men did not meet or solve. They met for prayer with the preacher before the morning service, parked cars, escorted seniors to their seats, and moved chairs when necessary. They were the hands of Aaron to Stan's Moses.

One such servant was Charlie. He was a mountain of a man who could lift an entire section of the platform by himself. His strength and prowess in construction were well known, and he felt a deep affinity for this pastor. There was virtually nothing he wouldn't do for him.

Except pray in public.

Charlie was the first to show up if there was a need, but he hated to take "center stage" in anything. Charlie had a sixth-grade education, and he felt his lack of knowledge debilitated him. He had felt skittish about coming to the church in work jeans and T-shirts, but when the preacher first greeted him, he did not even notice. Instead, Stan had welcomed him, enveloped him, and later discipled him after his conversion.

Charlie and Stan were an inseparable duo, often working late into the night, installing new speakers in the preschool department, or painting the youth room. Charlie's ability to build, fix, and improvise made him invaluable to the preacher, who could not drive a straight nail.

The one absolutely unbreakable caveat upon which Charlie insisted? "Never call on me to do anything publicly." And now, here was the pastor, asking Charlie to offer the prayer before the offering.

Certainly there was no malice behind the request. Stan had simply forgotten. His memory lapses were notorious in the church. He had even forgotten his own daughter's name during one memorable sermon illustration! Still, as silence enveloped the sanctuary, and you could hear the awkward shuffling of feet on the tile beneath the pews, Charlie gazed up at the preacher with the pleading look. "Please, call on someone else," his eyes seemed to plead.

But Stan had already lowered his head, and he never saw Charlie's fear.

The entire church did, however, and the awkward silence was broken by Charlie uttering, almost imperceptibly, a simple prayer out of frozen lips. After the "amen," the entire congregation exhaled together. The uncomfortable moment had passed. It had passed for everyone but Charlie.

Pastor Stanley's wife watched helplessly as Charlie walked by, red-faced, quickly taking the plate from one pew and passing another down the next aisle. After the money had been gathered, Charlie handed his plate to the man beside him, and then quietly walked out the back foyer, through the door, and to his car.

Charlie never entered another church again. All of Stanley's apologies and pleading did not change anything. Charlie was afflicted with the debilitating fear of speaking in public, and Stanley, however beguiling, had forced him to do just that. Charlie was paralyzed by a spiritual phobia.

Phobias Examined: A Paralysis of Faith

Regardless of your personal opinion about the psychobabble that seems to permeate Christian culture these days, most of us would agree that phobias are very real. They can freeze a person and limit his participation in any number of activities. Those who have a fear of a certain environment, such as crowds (agoraphobia), become paralyzed in that setting.

For instance, a child who is scared of the dark (scotophobia) begins to imagine every possible horrible scenario that can come from that encounter. Everything in his mind becomes focused not on his purpose (in this case sleep) or protection (a locked door, security, etc.) but on the danger involved.

In the Christian arena, a phobia will always limit a person's capacity to trust God, regardless of how strong he is in his Christian walk otherwise, because the phobia has developed into immense proportions. The task or calling becomes impossible, simply because it calls us into an arena beyond our security and safety. In effect, our fears put limits on the God who calls us.

Yet we must add that it is unreasonable to simply brush off another person's fears because they seem insignificant to us. Phobias seem to be as personal as they are debilitating. The Christian who encounters another Christian with a specific fear often "writes off" their fears as a lack of faith or a personal insecurity. The person with the specific fear immediately states that the other person does not understand, and may never understand, because he is uncaring. Thus, a cycle of misunderstanding develops. Yet the key to this dilemma seems to reside in the simple point that every person on the planet has some type of fear that, if pressed, would paralyze all of us as well.

In many ways, Ergun is an adrenaline junkie. He has parachuted, bungee jumped, parasailed, and scuba dived. On one occasion, he challenged his deacons at Wood Baptist Church in Franklin County, North Carolina, to a Bible study goal they had never achieved. The town of Wood had a population of 115, and though the worship attendance was equal to the town's population, the Bible study attendance was averaging only 60. So his challenge was this: If on Easter Sunday the church had at least 115 in Bible study, then he and his associate pastor (brother Emir) would parachute at the area airport.

Point of contention: Ergun has a fear of heights. Acrophobia.

Still, it seemed almost impossible. The church's highest recorded attendance had been 90—and remember, the town had a total population of 115.

On Easter Sunday 1995, they had 169 in Bible study.

The catch was, neither pastor was going to do any visitation. The entire onus was on the church body. They brought family members. They awakened sleeping neighbors. They stopped cars on the highway. The Raleigh CBS station traveled over ninety minutes to record the event. That afternoon, as the cameras rolled, the two brothers got up in the airplane and jumped 13,500 feet. Screaming all the way. Phobias can be conquered, right?

Wrong. Some can, but others appear insurmountable. Ergun cannot even walk if an insect buzzes past his ear. Frozen and paralyzed. Airplanes, yes. Bugs, no.

What may look like a simple issue to the uninitiated might immobilize the victim. If you do not believe us, ask Timothy.

The Hesitant Pastor: Timothy in Ephesus (2 Tim. 1)

In Paul's introduction to his young disciple in Ephesus, the letter begins with a normal salutation: "Paul, an apostle of Christ Jesus by God's will, for the promise of life in Christ Jesus: To Timothy, my dearly loved child. Grace, mercy, and peace from God the Father and Christ Jesus our Lord" (2 Tim. 1:1–2).

"Grace, mercy, and peace" are included in a variety of Paul's letters, and could not be distinguished from any other epistle he had written. Paul speaks of his calling ("by God's will") and his disciple ("my dearly loved child").

However, then Paul launched into a specific caution, aimed at Timothy and his own particular predilection. Paul reminded Timothy about his godly lineage, but he did so for a purpose.

I thank God, whom I serve with a clear conscience as
my forefathers did, when I constantly remember you in
my prayers night and day. Remembering your tears,
I long to see you so that I may be filled with joy, clearly
recalling your sincere faith that first lived in your
grandmother Lois, then in your mother Eunice, and
that I am convinced is in you also. (2 Tim. 1:3–5)

At first glance, Paul's words appear a bit out of place. About
which "tears" is Paul speaking? Why would Timothy's tears
cause Paul to want to return? Why would Timothy's godly
mother Eunice and godly grandmother Lois give Paul joy?

It seems somewhat capricious at first, until Paul gives his
reasoning for his words, proven by his transitional primary par-
ticle, *therefore*. This conjunction can be translated variously,
including "therefore," "indeed," and "for." In any case, the term
indicates that Paul was preparing to explain to Timothy why he
cited Timothy's family.

Timothy had a problem. Timothy had a fear that was trou-
bling his work for the Lord. Paul's specific citation to his son in
the ministry gently rebuked Timothy and his apparent lack of
strength in light of the church's problems. "Therefore, I remind
you to keep ablaze the gift of God that is in you through the laying on of my hands. For God has not given us a spirit of fearfulness, but one of power, love, and sound judgment" (2 Tim. 1:6–7).

The problem becomes very clear. The church, or the leadership of the church, was intimidating to Timothy. His response in
light of these problems: timidity. The term *fearfulness* is a transla-
tion of the Greek term *deilia*. *Deilia* can be translated as "fear,"
"timidity," "angst," or "fearfulness." In the face of a threat within
the fellowship, Timothy was responding by shrinking from the
challenge.

Perhaps Timothy had a fear of criticism (enissophobia).
Perhaps he did not like conflict. Perhaps Timothy was just
uncomfortable with arguing in general and responded by becoming mute. The specific reason may be vague, but Paul's inference
is clear. Timothy was responding to conflict with fear. He did not

stand for the truth he knew, and he had allowed the conflict to reduce his "blazing gift" to a dying ember.

Paul was a strong personality, to be sure. Yet Timothy's problem is not an insignificant one, nor is it isolated. If the law of averages holds true, roughly half of you can identify with Timothy. Like this young pastor, you also dislike confrontations, and when in conflict, your first response is to become introverted. In situations where Christ and his Word are challenged, you find yourself thinking that you should say something, but you rarely do.

In fact, one of the ways to know if you have a "Timothy" personality is that you often finish your arguments in your car alone driving home. Does that make sense? Have you ever found yourself making some salient point after the conflict, and wishing that you had the courage to speak? Take heart. Timothy is your forefather.

Compare Timothy to Titus

If Timothy was Paul's shrinking violet son, Titus was Paul's pugilist. Both are references by Paul as his "son." Notice his greeting in the opening of his epistle to him, "To Titus, my true child in our common faith" (Titus 1:4). Yet his reason for leaving Titus in Crete was to organize a people who were often unruly and unmanageable. Notice his next paragraph:

The reason I left you in Crete was to set right what was left undone and, as I directed you, to appoint elders in every town: someone who is blameless . . . having faithful children not accused of *wildness* or *rebellion*. For an overseer . . . must be blameless, not *arrogant*, not *quick tempered* . . . not a *bully* . . . but hospitable . . . *self-controlled*. . . . For there are also many *rebellious* people, idle talkers and deceivers. . . . It is necessary to silence them; they *overthrow whole households*. . . . One of their very own prophets said, Cretans are always *liars, evil*

beasts, lazy gluttons. This testimony is true. So, rebuke
them sharply, that they may be sound in the faith.
(Titus 1:5–14)

Review Paul's description of these leaders. Titus's task is
clear. Paul sent him to do what only Titus could do. Titus could
fight with the best of them. Paul even cited the Cretan poet
Epimenides (sixth century BC), and called those who lived in
Crete "liars" and "evil beasts." Later in the chapter, he adds,
"They profess to know God, but they deny Him by their works.
They are detestable, disobedient, and disqualified for any good
work." (Titus 1:16)

Titus was up to the task. His problem, however, was that he
was impetuous himself. Titus, from all indications, liked to argue
and fight as well. Look at Paul's warnings to Titus later in the
epistle:

But you must speak what is consistent with sound
teaching. Older men are to be self-controlled, worthy of
respect, sensible, and sound in faith, love, and
endurance. (Titus 2:1–2)

Set an example of good works yourself, with integrity
and dignity in your teaching. Your message is to be sound
beyond reproach, so that the opponent will be ashamed,
having nothing bad to say about us. (Titus 2:7–8)

But avoid foolish debates, genealogies, quarrels,
and disputes about the law, for they are unprofitable
and worthless. Reject a divisive person after a first and
second warning, knowing that such a person is per-
verted and sins, being self-condemned. (Titus 3:9–11)

Fear was not Titus's problem. The situation was different for
Timothy. The inevitable conflicts that both Timothy and Titus
faced must have made Timothy's stomach knot incessantly. His
timidity is understandable, given his personal inclinations, but
the situation was not hopeless. Neither is it for you.

Perhaps your fear may be of a different variation. Perhaps
you have a fear of speaking to your friends about Christ because
you fear looking foolish. Perhaps you fear their mockery.

Perhaps you fear stepping out in faith into some new adventure, because you secretly fear that it will all come crashing down, and you will be left without money or a job. Perhaps you fear change, because your security is based on patterns and routines.

Fears, even fears of insignificant things, are equally incapacitating. Both the Old and New Testaments are filled with those for whom fear served as a blockade. In some cases, fear can kill. David understood the depths of fear when he wrote, "Fear and trembling grip me; horror has overwhelmed me" (Ps. 55:5). Proverbs also speaks to the issue when it says, "The fear of man is a snare, but the one who trusts in the LORD is protected" (Prov. 29:25).

The disciples understood fear, especially when Christ appeared to them, walking on the water: "When the disciples saw Him walking on the sea, they were terrified. 'It's a ghost!' they said, and cried out in fear" (Matt. 14:26). On the first Easter morning, the guards at the borrowed tomb discovered Christ's resurrection, and the Bible tells us, "The guards were so shaken from fear of him that they became like dead men" (Matt. 28:4).

Remember this: Any fear that causes you to stop serving God or modify your direction in any way is *sin*. The only limits to God's use of your gifts are the limits you impose yourself. Paul was not speaking as someone who was removed from the condition of fear either. Notice his words to the Corinthian church: "And I was with you in weakness, in fear, and in much trembling" (1 Cor. 2:3).

The Solution to Phobic Christianity

The solution is found in Paul's encouragement to Timothy. God does not haphazardly tell us to "get over it" and then send us into the terror of our hearts. In fact, the answer may surprise you. Godly fear can cast away ungodly phobias.

Of the number of uses of the term *fear* in Scripture, many are used in the positive sense. "Fear of the Lord" is not a phobic kind of anxiety and dread but a godly reverence. This type of fear is a healthy respect and worship. It is recognition that God is God, and we are his creation. It recognizes that he has the power over life and death, and that if we are to be humbled, we are to be humbled by him. Notice Paul's teaching to the church at Corinth in his second letter: "Therefore dear friends, since we have such promises, we should wash ourselves clean from every impurity of the flesh and spirit, making our sanctification complete in the fear of God" (2 Cor. 7:1).

Fear, in this instance, actually enables us to complete our sanctification, since this type of fear motivates us to serve the God who saved us and called us. This type of fear, also translated from the Greek term *phobos*, motivates us to godly action, rather than paralyzing us in terror. The motivation for a Christian is not a terror that drives us from something; we are motivated by a love that drives us toward our Father. The apostle John says, "There is no fear in love; instead, perfect love drives out fear, because fear involves punishment. So the one who fears has not reached perfection in love" (1 John 4:18).

Second, fear's paralysis can seriously jeopardize the vital kingdom work that each generation faces. In fact, Paul's words of support to Timothy carried with them the implication that if Timothy remained frozen in inaction, then the damage would be severe, and the cost would be dear.

Hold on to the pattern of sound teaching that you have heard from me, in the faith and love that are in Christ Jesus. Guard, through the Holy Spirit who lives in us, that good thing entrusted to you. This you know: all those in Asia have turned away from me, including Phygelus and Hermogenes. (2 Tim. 1:13–15)

Reject foolish and ignorant disputes, knowing that they breed quarrels. The Lord's slave must not quarrel, but must be gentle to everyone, able to teach, and patient, instructing his opponents with gentleness. Perhaps God will grant them repentance to know the truth. Then they may come to their senses and escape the Devil's trap, having been captured by him to do his will. (2 Tim. 2:23–26)

Before God and Christ Jesus, who is going to judge the living and the dead, and by His appearing and His kingdom, I solemnly charge you: proclaim the message; persist in it whether convenient or not; rebuke, correct, and encourage with great patience and teaching. For the time will come when they will not tolerate sound doctrine, but according to their own desires, will accumulate teachers for themselves because they have an itch to hear something new. They will turn away from hearing the truth and will turn aside to myths. But as for you, keep a clear head about everything, endure hardship, do the work of an evangelist, fulfill your ministry. (2 Tim. 4:1–5)

Paul's words to Timothy were clear. Eternal consequences hang in the balance. Within the church, there will be those who rise up and challenge the truth of the Scripture. If Timothy did not speak up, church members would follow lies, perpetuated by those like Phygelus and Hermogenes. In addition, Paul explained that Timothy would *fulfill* his ministry by clearly and strongly proclaiming the Bible, regardless of consequence.

Paul offered one final piece of encouragement. Though the persecution Timothy feared was both serious and daunting, Paul reminded Timothy that persecution was the standard for those who follow Christ. The fear of ridicule is unfounded, because ridicule was normative for all who stand for Christ. Paul wrote, "So don't be ashamed of the testimony about our Lord, or of me His prisoner. Instead, *share in suffering for the gospel,* relying on the power of God" (2 Tim. 1:8).

Therefore, if the old proverb, "Fear makes a wolf bigger than he is," is true, then our various phobias are actually evidence that the devil is attempting to do everything he can to stop your work. If the devil cannot rob you of your salvation and your effectiveness, then he will work to silence you. Fears, phobias, and neuroses are some of his most effective means.

Chapter 11

Anorexia and Bulimia: Eating Disorders of the Word of God

The Hebrew Church, Milk, and Meat
Hebrews 5:11–14

At twelve o'clock noon, every Sunday, she got up and walked out of church.

It was like clockwork. Every Sunday, for as long as anyone could remember, Darlene would check her watch during the sermon. Regardless of the pastor, regardless of the special event, regardless of the weather, she would impatiently check her watch. Precisely at noon, Darlene would gather her things, stand to her feet, and slip out down the aisle and out the door. No one ever questioned her about it. They didn't have to.

Darlene would tell anyone who would listen about her habit of leaving. "From 10 AM until noon, we are on God's time. After that, the preacher is on my time." Through the years, pastors would speak of her habit as quenching the Spirit. They would encourage her to stay through the invitation, so as to not disturb others who were listening to the preaching.

She would have nothing of it. Darlene would become impatient when the topic came up. "The Holy Spirit does not have to be long-winded," she would say. "If you plan the sermon and the service right, you'll have enough time," she would conclude with a stern nod.

Some people remembered a confrontation that Darlene had with an evangelist. Approximately twenty years ago, an evangelist was holding a protracted meeting at the church, and everyone who was around then remembered the service. By Thursday night, the evangelist had had his fill of Darlene stepping out precisely at 8:00 PM. As soon as he saw her stand and turn, the evangelist rushed to the back door, dramatically threw his Bible on the carpet in front of the door, and exclaimed, "Sister, if you are going to walk out in a huff, you are going to have to walk over the Word of God!"

Darlene looked at the Bible for a moment, stepped to the right, and walked around the Bible on her way out the door. The surviving members remembered that she had a sly grin on her face as she walked calmly and steadily down to her car. You could hear a pin drop as the evangelist shuffled to the pulpit, awkwardly, and concluded his sermon quickly.

Darlene was back the next night, sitting in her place, as if nothing had happened.

Though most of the members of our churches would never be as adamant as Darlene, many would applaud her tenacity. They would agree with her rationale and her thinking. Longtime Christians, who have served in churches for decades, wonder what all the fuss is about when it comes to sermons. Why do pastors complain when members gently remind them that they are going longer than they need to go? Is it so wrong to want church to be accessible to everyone these days, especially with schedules being so tight and everyone being so busy? Wouldn't more people come to church if they knew that the service would fit into their schedules?

Welcome to the contemporary church. We sing. We worship. We meet.

And we have a spiritual eating disorder. We have a revulsion to the meat of the Word of God.

The Contemporary Church and Young Saints

As a pastor, Mac has seen three generations of church members. In one church, he ended up with a finance committee chairman who did not tithe. The man freely admitted such, and the budget process that year was a fiasco. When the pastor approached the man who had recommended the man to the position, he discovered an amazing piece of illogical church logic. The man who nominated the non-giver to the committee believed that by doing so, it would make him more faithful!

This is somewhat akin to hiring an anorexic to be a chef! No wonder the church was struggling. It was being led by people who rejected the Bible defiantly, and then called the people who were following to faithfulness.

As a professor, Ergun has seen seventeen-year-old Christian youth enter his classrooms, ready to begin the university experience. They have been Christians for a number of years, and many have been very active in their youth groups. They wear shirts with logos from the latest Christian bands and can sing along with the most detailed lyrics. They can passionately defend their faith, and most of them can lead a friend to Christ. They love missions, they love souls, and they love Jesus.

The problem is, most of them would have a problem distinguishing between Malachi and Matthew.

It is not their fault; it is ours. For twenty years, since the second "Jesus Revolution" movement of the mid-1980s, our churches have fed them a steady diet of "lite" sermons. As our churches exploded in growth and we became focused on trends and movements, one of the first "traditions" to be jettisoned was the clichéd long and winding sermon. Our pulpits began to confuse relevance with truth. We began to expound sermons on "Fifteen Reasons to Get Up Tomorrow" and "Thirty Ways to Get Over a Heartache."

We decided that people needed truth in small doses, and we left the heavier and deeper truths for small groups, cell groups, and Discipleship Training. The problem is that the Christian audience in general developed an aversion to the most profound and deep truths of Scripture.

In addition, the worship experience also exploded on our culture. Hundreds of thousands of young Christians have attended thousands of concerts and meetings, and their praises have reached the heavens. Truly, Christian music and worship have entered the mainstream, and bands have become our new heroes. Sadly, many of these bands are so talented that the last component they consider are the lyrics. They find a Christian songwriter, a good beat, and three chords, and the next thing you know, they are headlining.

Tragically, as these youth look up to these bands as their spiritual mentors, many of the bands are starved for the Word of God as well. They are so busy traveling and playing, they rarely have time to attend church, much less get deeper in their biblical knowledge and wisdom. Thus, the milk-fed musicians are writing milk-fed songs, and feeding spiritually lactose-intolerant youth.

Please take note that these are not the words of two elderly curmudgeons, whining that things are "not the way they used to be!" Both authors not only speak in youth conferences and events, but Ergun commits ten weeks a year to youth camps and events. We have a passionate commitment to youth and college-age Christians and have spoken at state fairs and amusement parks, as well as civic auditoriums. We share the stage with the very people and the very culture we are discussing.

You see, it is not the musicians' fault either. They are also victims of a culture that demands results, releases, and success. The Christian carousel is spinning faster and faster, and yet not getting anywhere. If we are not careful, we will become casualties of our own popularity. The Christian culture's fame will become our poison. We will encounter an entire generation of Christian leaders who have developed spiritual anorexia and bulimia.

Spiritual Anorexia and Bulimia Explained

The afflictions of anorexia and bulimia are no light-hearted matter. Young men and women become afflicted by the psychosis when, faced with a poor body image, they willfully starve themselves until their bodies are depleted of every nutrient. If left unabated, the victim will die from complications related to anorexia and bulimia.

In the spiritual realm, Christians who suffer from anorexia and bulimia are actually slowly starved to death in the passive sense. One of the markers of salvation is a hunger and thirst for God's Word. At the embryonic stages of Christianity, the young convert devours the Bible, usually reading copious amounts of Scripture at each setting. The Bible is new and alive, full of promises and hope. The narratives of God's intervention in history and intercession for his children are amazing. They cannot get enough.

Then, slowly and imperceptibly, the initial thrust of interest begins to ebb. Perhaps it is when they hit the book of Leviticus, and they bog down in the legal constraints for various diseases. Perhaps it was when they could not keep the northern kingdom kings and the southern kingdom kings straight. Whatever the case, they cut back on the number of chapters they read daily.

Perhaps it is because they run into other lackadaisical members.

One young man in Kentucky came forward in his church one Sunday. His entire youth group had been praying for him. The youth pastor had been speaking to him about salvation. Until that Sunday, he had been reluctant because he felt it was too good to be true. That Sunday, however, he was saved. As he stood before the church and the pastor presented him to the church body, tears streamed down his face. He was released and relieved. Finally the burden of sin had been lifted. He was excited.

After the service, the members filed by, shaking his hand and welcoming him into the fellowship. One lady took a Polaroid shot of him and they put it in the old wooden hymn plaque in the foyer. The people were friendly and congratulatory, and he felt like he had a family. Then an elderly woman whom everyone called "Aunt Louise" walked by and shook his hand.

"Are you crying, my dear?" she asked.

"Yes, Ma'am," he answered. "I am just so happy to be saved!"

She smiled a small smile, and said, "Well, you'll get over it."

Perhaps that is the problem. We allow people to "get over" their love for Jesus and his Word.

Hebrews: Lactose-Intolerant Babes in Christ (Heb. 5:11–14)

All the spiritual eating disorders begin in a small manner. The development of an allergic reaction to the milk of the Word takes time, and only after time does it become noticeable. Christians who should be strong and vibrant become stunted in their spiritual growth, and the cause is clear. They have neglected the steady diet of the Bible.

The process of Christian growth through the nourishment of the Word is seen nowhere more clearly than in the book of Hebrews. The author (perhaps Paul) is gently chiding the church for its spiritual apathy and diminutive faith. In chapter 5 of the book, he summarizes their ailment and details what the normative growth should be:

We have a great deal to say about this, and it's difficult to explain, since you have become slow to understand. For though by this time you ought to be teachers, you need someone to teach you again the basic principles of God's revelation. You need milk, not solid food. Now everyone who lives on milk is inexperienced with the message about righteousness, because he is an infant.

But solid food is for the mature — for those whose
senses have been trained to distinguish between good
and evil (Heb. 5:11–14).

Notice the author's rationale for his rebuke of the church:

- They had much to learn but could not.
- Their predicament was difficult to explain because they
  were slow to understand.
- By this time, many of them should be discipling other
  Christians, but instead they themselves needed someone
  to walk them through the basics in the Bible.
- They could not handle the deeper and more profound
  issues of Christianity. Instead, they needed the basic
  "milk," which was easily digested and simple in formula.
- "Milk-fed Christians" are unable to handle the doctrines
  and profundity of God, because they are spiritual infants.
- "Solid food," the true meat of the Word, is only for mature
  Christians.
- "Solid food" is for those who have developed spiritual wisdom and discernment, knowing right and wrong without
  having it fed to them in the passive sense.

Thus, we get a window into the life of this desperate church.
They were an immature fellowship that had been swept up in any
number of erroneous teachings. The resolution to these theological problems was almost impossible, however, because they first
needed to get the basics settled. They were unable to digest the
deeper things of God and instead could only handle the very
rudimentary issues of Christianity. Intense study was beyond
them, because for Christians to get deeper they must mature in
their walk. One of the marks of Christian maturity is the ability
to distinguish between truth and error, as well as biblical truths
and unbiblical deceptions.

Recognize anyone in that description?

Some Christian students enter our Christian universities and
seminaries, and immediately they have a difficult time in classes,
because their understanding of the essential and fundamental
elements of Christianity is flawed. They have only an experiential

understanding of Christ. We are not doubting their salvation; we are lamenting their lack of maturity.

Neither are we blaming the pastors or churches completely. The blame for our predicament is spread evenly throughout the contemporary Christian world. Churches make demands on the pastors to "go easy," because they cannot handle the "meat." Pastors notice that churches grow when they preach less intensive, less demanding sermons. Offerings go up when we keep everyone happy. We hear of church growth methods that make a sustainable play for discipleship, but only for a radically small percentage of the body. We begin to form the assumption that maturity in Christ and his Word is not for everyone.

We are deadly wrong.

The consequences of Christian immaturity are dire. Every year in every church, we receive reports of new members (and sometimes older members) being carried away into a cult. Our churches begin to fight over issues that are clearly settled in the Word of God, simply because the members (and sometimes the leaders) do not know the Bible. Thus, they act on feeling and experience. Churches adopt unbiblical standards and doctrines, and no one is the wiser, because they have never discovered the truths in serious and systematic Bible study.

As this pattern continues, the problem becomes even more pandemic. These spiritually immature, milk-fed Christians rise to positions of leadership. The church, confusing man's talents for God's gifting, sees certain attributes in these people that would make them effective leaders. But without a foundation in the Bible, these new leaders begin teaching, and they can take their classes and their students only as far and as deep as they themselves are. Thus, the milk-fed teachers try to bring their converts to their level, but even that shallow depth is too much. The second generation of shallow Christians becomes lactose-intolerant. They cannot even handle the very basic issues.

Something has to fill their need. Something has to satiate their hunger and thirst for righteousness. Where truth, doctrine, and Scripture cannot fill, experience enters. The generation of superficial Christians then begins to measure their Christianity, not by what they believe but by how they feel.

This is a profound error. Measuring your Christianity by your experience can lead to a myriad of related ailments. Without a true biblical marker and measurement, one is easily deceived into measuring by the amount of tears one cries or the sharpness of the tingle that transverses your spine.

This condition is made worse when we realize that our culture measures truth by the same standards. Think about it. These days, it is rare to find anyone use the phrase, "I believe." Rational thought is scorned in the marketplace. Instead, it has been replaced with the phrase, "I feel." The person speaking develops a serious look on his face. He attempts to look genuine as he feeds you his rationale for his position. Regardless of how ungodly his belief system is, he will attempt to convince you of its *authenticity* because of his *sincerity.*

Therefore, *sincerity* becomes the measuring standard for truth. Unfortunately, people can be both sincere and sincerely *wrong.* Hitler was sincere. That did not make him right.

Enter the worship dilemma. Musicians, many of whom are actually very mature Christians, discover that a generation of lactose-intolerant Christian youth cannot and will not imbibe deep theological and biblical truths in their music. Though the artists attempt to disciple the youth with weighty teachings, these truths go right over their heads. Instead, sensory-measuring youth seek sensory-satisfying worship. *Does the song make me cry? Does the melody make me jump up and down? Is it a catchy tune?* Then it will become a big hit, whether or not the words make sense.

Currently, a popular Christian group of singers has had great success at crossing over into both the Southern Gospel and Contemporary Christian markets. Their concerts sell out, and their albums are best sellers. Unfortunately, all the members of this group come from a Christian sect that has cultic tendencies, such as teaching that their sect alone is going to heaven. Still, the people will say, "Stop talking about it. Those types of discussions divide and separate. We need to be united."

Still another Christian author and speaker was raised in a sect that denies the Trinity. Though there is some question about whether he himself denies the Father, Son, and Holy Spirit, his ministry clearly proclaims that they believe in "one God and three manifestations of God."

Read that again.

Does that phrase bother you? Or is your first response to jump to their defense and say we should focus on what "unites us, rather than what divides us"? Do you believe that the denial of the Trinity is acceptable within the scope of Christian teaching and culture? What if they do not outright deny the Trinity, but instead they are "fuzzy" on the matter, maintaining a balance between clarity and opacity?

And yet this particular Christian author and speaker is one of the most popular in America. We are a Christian culture that has grown accustomed to lactose intolerance.

The symptoms of spiritual infancy (and being "milk-fed") are the same for physical infancy. They cannot feed themselves but are wholly dependent on others for nourishment. They can take the "milk" only in small doses. Perhaps most telling, they cry when their needs are not met, because of their total self-centeredness. How can they even consider others when they themselves have a need for constant attention?

The Bulimic Church: Purging (2 Tim. 4:1–5)

In the spiritual arena, bulimia precedes anorexia. In the physical world, they can be separate. In this sphere, spiritual bulimia develops when the average Christian has taken the nourishment and received the Word of God, only to forcibly purge themselves of it. They reject the "meat" because they do not like it.

Listen to Paul's admonition to his son, Timothy, about a bulimic church:

Before God and Christ Jesus, who is going to judge the living and the dead, and by His appearing and His kingdom, I solemnly charge you: proclaim the message; persist in it whether convenient or not; rebuke, correct, and encourage with great patience and teaching. For the time will come when they will not tolerate sound doctrine, but according to their own desires, will accumulate teachers for themselves because they have an itch to hear something new. They will turn away from hearing the truth and will turn aside to myths. But as for you, keep a clear head about everything, endure hardship, do the work of an evangelist, fulfill your ministry. (2 Tim. 4:1–5)

They will not tolerate the message because they cannot tolerate the message. They reject it because it does not satisfy their craving. They crave what is easy to digest and experientially moving. They want something "new," and the Bible will not do.

When the pastor or teacher attempts to preach the whole counsel of God, the people almost immediately choose to reject this teaching. Perhaps they will say you preach too long. Perhaps they will say that you are going over everyone's heads. Yet in the end, they will purge the teaching, no matter how you package it, because their spiritual bodies cannot tolerate it.

Paul compares this type of rejection to the response of the Jewish nation to the resurrected Christ. In his sermon recorded in Acts 13, Paul states, "It was necessary that God's message be spoken to you first. But since you reject it, and consider yourselves unworthy of eternal life, we now turn to the Gentiles!" (Acts 13:46).

Yet to Timothy, Paul is emphatic. You must preach it anyway. To all the teachers and preachers and songwriters who bemoan the lack of acceptance of the teaching of the truths of Scripture, Paul says, "Preach it anyway. Teach it anyway. Endure the hardship that comes from such a stand, because in so doing, you are fulfilling your calling."

The Anorexic Church: Rejecting

The natural consequence of the sin of spiritual bulimia is eventual anorexia. The Christian or church that continually rejects discipleship through the Word of God will eventually develop not only an intolerance for it, but an outright rejection of it.

David speaks of his frustration with an anorexic Israelite nation in Psalm 119 when he says, "Rage seizes me because of the wicked who reject Your instruction" (Ps. 119:53). Could the words of God in Hosea also be directed to the Christians and churches who accept only a steady diet of spiritual junk food? "My people are destroyed for lack of knowledge. Because you have rejected knowledge, I will reject you from serving as My priest. Since you have forgotten the law of your God, I will also forget your sons" (Hos. 4:6).

Have you ever considered this lack of knowledge? Did the sons of Judah, to whom Hosea was speaking, lack knowledge because it was not being provided, or because they were rejecting what was offered?

Thankfully, both spiritual bulimia and anorexia are curable. The process of teaching these Christians is slow, but it is possible. Across our nation, there are testimonies of churches that have learned to relish in the Word and have developed great ministries based on truth and meat. At times the process was painful for many of them, and some of the bulimic and anorexic leaders left the church. But the end result of this "back door revival" was a deepening of the body and a security in God and his Word.

The people eventually developed a healthful appetite for God's Word, and the ironic consequence is this: their worship shows it! The singing remained joyous and the music remained buoyant, but the worship experience became even more emphatic and meaningful. The principle? *You cannot have good doxology without good theology.*

Let us take to heart the concluding words of the writer of Hebrews in relation to this issue. The problem can be solved, and the ailment is curable. God has called us to "move on to maturity." "Therefore, leaving the elementary message about the Messiah, let us go on to maturity, not laying again the foundation of repentance from dead works, faith in God, teaching about ritual washings, laying on of hands, the resurrection of the dead, and eternal judgment" (Heb. 6:1–2).

Chapter 12

Hypochondria:
The Gift of Discouragement

Demas and the Ministry of Misery
2 Timothy 4:9–13

The Sunday service was everything for which Pastor Stevens had prayed. Having worked for months to ensure that everything would go smoothly, he had begun that day with a touch of anxiety. *Did we cover everything?* he thought, as he dressed quickly to get to the church. The preparation for the first day of the revival had been like the planning of the D-Day landing at Normandy. Visitations, fliers, advertising—all had been done in the preceding weeks. Cottage prayer meetings in the homes of deacons and Bible study teachers had been most profitable, as the people sought the face of God. Every event, every venue possible, seemingly had been covered.

In addition, the church had received a fresh coat of paint in the auditorium, and a "Saturday church clean-up" had spruced up the exterior of the church grounds. With the number of visitors they were anticipating, the church members wanted the facilities to look as good as possible.

As an added blessing, the youth had taken it upon themselves to cover the city with posters, announcing the revival services, complete with a picture of the evangelist on the front. The two months of preparation for the services would culminate this morning. Pastor Stevens silently prayed as the hour approached.

Following the service, the pastor silently chided himself for his lack of faith. God had truly visited the church that morning. The pastor should not have been surprised. The choir and praise team sounded magnificent. The auditorium was packed. Visitors were everywhere. The preacher had really given a word from God, and a large number of people had come forward at the invitation to accept Jesus Christ as Lord. The pastor was giddy with joy.

Until . . .

Out of the corner of his eye he saw her coming down the hall. Her gait was unmistakable, and he had long ago learned to listen for her voice, always saying the same thing:

"Preacher, I really need to speak to you for a minute."

Pastor Stevens paused a moment as he fumbled with the keys, locking up the church office. His mind raced, and for a brief moment, he considered acting like he had not heard her. Perhaps he could duck back into the office and lock the door.

No, not on a day like today, he finally said to himself. Even *she* could not ruin a day like this.

Clara had been a member of Pastor Stevens's church for decades. She was a fixture in the fellowship. And over the span of that time, she had developed quite a reputation among the members. She was a high-maintenance member. To use the current vernacular, she was a "buzz kill." No one had the capacity to complain like Clara.

"Preacher, I need to speak to you," she said again. "I prayed about whether I should even bring this up, but I feel that the Lord would want me to."

The pastor held his breath, knowing that those words were always the beginning of a rebuke.

"I came this morning to be blessed," she continued. "I really did. But as I came in the church this morning, I could not believe my eyes. Some visitors were sitting in my pew—preacher, my pew. You know that with my condition, I have to sit in that pew to enjoy the service."

The pastor exhaled slightly and spoke.

"Clara, I know that pew was purchased . . ."

Before he could finish the sentence, she interrupted.

"And you know that pew was purchased by my mother and father in 1943, and our family has been seated in that pew for over sixty years . . ."

Her voice trailed off, as she turned her head to the side. Pastor Stevens knew what was coming next. He had heard it countless times.

"Why, I can still picture my dear husband, sitting there, God rest his soul. Until he died in 1973, he would always sit there, looking so handsome."

"Yes, Clara, I have heard what a wonderful man he was," the pastor said softly. For thirty years, Clara had brought up her family as a type of "trump card." No one could top her on the sympathy list, because she always held it until just the right time. Now, with the cards on the table, she continued a bit more strongly than before.

"And to see strangers seated in his pew . . . well, it just broke my heart."

The pastor gazed through the church office window, wondering if he should even make the effort to give a rebuttal. The evangelist was sitting just outside the office door in the parking lot, in the pastor's car.

"Well, Clara, that entire family joined the church this morning. Isn't that wonderful? Don't you think your parents would be pleased?" He attempted to buoy her spirits, but it was to no avail. Clara was determined to finish her rebuke. She leaned toward him as she spoke, her small, frail frame pulled to its maximum height as she pointed her finger.

"And then, Pastor, when I opened the bulletin, my heart was just broken."

Clara removed the bulletin from her Bible, which was brimming with what looked like hundreds of bulletins from previous services.

She continued, dramatically. "Look here, Pastor. I dedicated the flowers on the Lord's Supper table to the memory of my mother and father, and you misspelled their names! I have been dedicating the flowers in the sanctuary in their memory for years. Why did you do that?"

The pastor attempted to explain that the secretary had made an honest error, but he could not even begin his apology. She continued emphatically.

"Why, I have even considered leaving the church. The insult was just too much to bear. And with me, having this gout, I have been so weak lately. Yesterday, I couldn't even get out of bed. And I called the office, but I could not get a hold of you. I really needed a visit. You visited me on Monday, but yesterday the pain in my arm came back, and I thought I was going to have to go to the emergency room, and then I do everything I can to get up and come to the Lord's house, and I am personally insulted."

In Pastor Stevens's mind, Clara's voice trailed off into so much background noise. He had long since learned to maintain eye contact when she would begin her litany of ailments and alleged insults. Yet his mind would wander. It was not that he was uncaring or unconcerned. It was just that he could almost repeat her speech, word for word.

In the twenty years he had been at the church, Pastor Stevens had never known a day when Clara was happy. Or well. Or positive. She was a walking complaint department. Sometimes she would highlight and circle the misspellings in the bulletin. Sometimes she would rise to say that the church was too hot. Or too cold. Or too breezy, whatever that meant.

She would complain about the music being too loud, or the service being too long. She would lament that the janitor had not cleaned the church properly, or that the church had a "funny smell." God help the member or visitor who dared park in what she perceived as "her parking spot." One time, he thought she was going to have a stroke when he proposed changing the hours of the worship service to accommodate another service that was needed due to growth. Clara had long since stopped coming on Wednesday nights, but that did not stop her from objecting loudly when the church attempted to add a fellowship supper before Wednesday night prayer meeting. Even though she did not attend Wednesday nights, that did not stop her from having one of her friends read her list of requests. She would get one of them to bring the list, and every Sunday she checked the bulletin to see that her requests had been added.

Clara also never met an excuse or ailment she did not like. She could not drive to church at night because of her eyes. That did not stop her, apparently, from driving all over town in the evening, if the feeling suited her. She demanded to be visited every week, but she was never satisfied. The pastor always made sure to stay long enough, because if he just dropped by for a quick visit, she would be offended, and she would tell every member within earshot.

On the week his third child was born, he had missed his weekly visit because his wife was in the hospital. Clara was inconsolable. She spoke of perceived insults and slights that had happened decades ago, as if they had just happened that week. Clara never forgot.

Yet her memory of good and blessed events seemed to be limited. Virtually every major revival, every visitation of God's presence in that church, was marred in her memory by some affront. To Pastor Stevens, no person in the world was more skilled at snatching *defeat* from the jaws of *victory* than Clara. Every time she spoke, he could feel his blood pressure rising.

It would be different, or somehow lessened, if Clara were not so high-maintenance. She was not just satisfied reveling in her own misery; she went out of her way to pull others into her misery as well. She marinated in her melancholy, simmering slowly for hours, awaiting the moment when she could tell someone about her latest sorrow. She demanded her friends' attention. When they did not call her, she was insulted. When she called them and they were not home, she was wounded. She was saturated in her feelings of passive-aggressive anger. "No," she often said to friends offering to lend an ear, "I don't want to burden you."

But she did. Pastor Stevens attempted to steal a look at his watch, but he was sure she would notice. Secretly, he wished someone would call his cell phone so he could excuse himself. Then he felt guilty about his thoughts. *Am I becoming too calloused?* he wondered. He remembered that earlier in the week, when she called his house, he hesitated when he saw her name come up on caller ID. He stood and stared at the phone for a moment, contemplating picking up the receiver, until he finally did, on the sixth ring.

Finally, Pastor Stevens broke from his daydream and spoke cheerfully.

"Well Clara, I know it has been a rough time for you, but isn't it exciting that over thirty people were saved this morning?"

Clara did not miss a beat. The pastor wondered if she had even heard him. In truth, he doubted if she would even care if three *hundred* souls had been saved that day. It mattered little to Clara. The only thing that mattered to her was her problem-laden life.

Clara was a spiritual hypochondriac. She was high-maintenance.

Spiritual Hypochondria

In the medical field, hypochondriacs are people who believe they are ill, sick, and dying from a variety of ailments. Every day a new set of circumstances brings them to believe that their condition is worsening, and they are gravely ill, if not terminal. The medical community believes it is a psychological problem, and that the symptoms are all in the victim's head.

In our world, spiritual hypochondria is a heart issue. It is the condition of Christians who are only happy when they are miserable. They are members of the church who move from crisis to crisis and achieve unbelievable levels of drama in their lives.

At first, their unsuspecting Christian friends are sympathetic to their plight, and they listen for hours as the spiritual hypochondriac pours out his or her pains, conspiracies, and calamities. Then, slowly, almost subtly, they begin to notice a pattern. This person is never joyful. He is never satisfied. He has developed the capacity to complain in the midst of bounty and blessing. He is a hypochondriac.

We are sure you have them in your church.

You are thinking of that person right now.

They are "life-drainers," and you are getting bemused and tired just thinking about them.

The Apostle Paul's Hypochondriac: Demas

The Bible is full of illustrations of those who relished their own troubles. One of the Bible's most mysterious characters may have been its biggest hypochondriac. He certainly was a fair-weather friend. His name is Demas.

As the apostle Paul set out on his missionary endeavors, he developed friendships across the Middle Eastern world. Aquila and Priscilla, also examined in this book, were his comrades in Ephesus, for example. These people often gave Paul a bed and comfort when he passed through.

He also developed a band of fellow travelers and missionaries who joined him in starting churches and building the kingdom. They became his inner circle. However, just as our Lord was betrayed by one of his disciples, Paul also had trouble with his friends. As Judas was to Christ, Demas was to Paul.

Though he is mentioned only three times in the Bible, Demas appears at the most poignant of moments. During Paul's first imprisonment in Rome (AD 60–63), he wrote four letters that would become part of the New Testament: Ephesians, Philippians, Colossians, and Philemon.

In two of those epistles, Paul took special time to mention those who were serving with him, even under house arrest. Notice what he wrote to Philemon: "Epaphras, my fellow prisoner in Christ Jesus, greets you, and so do Mark, Aristarchus, Demas, and Luke, my co-workers. The grace of the Lord Jesus Christ be with your spirit" (Philem. 23–25).

Among the list of five men that Paul cites, Demas is the fourth one. Along with the others, he is called a "fellow worker," which conveys a sense of camaraderie and friendship. Certainly they would have to be especially good and dear friends to work with a man who had been sentenced to serve time for criminal behavior.

Some might speculate that Epaphras was the only friend who was in lockdown with Paul, because he makes the distinction between Epaphras ("fellow prisoner") and the other four ("fellow workers"). Such a distinction is speculative at best. All five were actually in Paul's presence, and he sent greetings on their behalf.

In his epistle to the Colossians, Paul included more details at the conclusion about his friends in arms:

Aristarchus, my fellow prisoner, greets you, as does Mark, Barnabas' cousin (concerning whom you have received instructions: if he comes to you, welcome him), and so does Jesus who is called Justus. These alone of the circumcision are my co-workers for the kingdom of God, and they have been a comfort to me. Epaphras, who is one of you, a slave of Christ Jesus, greets you. He is always contending for you in his prayers, so that you can stand mature and fully assured in everything God wills. For I testify about him that he works hard for you, for those in Laodicea, and for those in Hierapolis. Luke, the loved physician, and Demas greet you. (Col. 4:10–14)

The addition of one other member of his group, Justus, adds the detail that Demas was not Jewish, though his name could have been evidence of that as well. Demas is a contraction of the Greek name *Demetrius*. Again, however, Demas joined Paul in sending greetings to the sister church.

How active was Demas in the Lord's work? It is interesting that in Colossians, Paul took great pains to detail the labor of Mark, Justus, and Epaphras. Demas was simply mentioned in connection with Paul's term of sentence in Rome. No statement of his work. No elucidation of his labor in the kingdom on their behalf. He is just there.

While we should not use silence as the measure for any conclusion, Paul's words in his final letter leave no room for question. He wrote:

Make every effort to come to me soon, for Demas has deserted me, because he loved this present world, and has gone to Thessalonica. Crescens has gone to Galatia, Titus to Dalmatia. Only Luke is with me. Bring Mark with you, for he is useful to me in the ministry. I have sent Tychicus to Ephesus. When you come, bring the cloak I left in Troas with Carpus, as well as the scrolls, especially the parchments. (2 Tim. 4:9–13)

During his final imprisonment, chained before two guards and awaiting certain death, Paul expounded about his lonely state. Crescens had gone to Galatia, and Titus to Dalmatia. Tychicus had gone to Timothy's town of Ephesus, and Mark was there as well. Paul asked that Timothy and Mark come to give him comfort and to bring a coat and his books.

It sounds like everyone was gone, serving the Lord in various cities, with one exception. Paul reserved one detail about Demas that he did not add to the others—a rebuke. Read the text again: "Demas has deserted me, because he loved this world, and has gone to Thessalonica."

What happened? Was Demas simply tired, and he decided to retire? Did he feel compelled to serve God on the field? Both options seem implausible, given Paul's words. Demas "deserted" Paul. His reason for doing so was that he "loved this present world." Demas stood with Paul through his first imprisonment, and one would hope that now, approximately four years later, he would remain with his traveling companion, but he did not. He left. Not for spiritual reasons and not for familial emergencies. He deserted Paul. His faith was a "fair weather" variety. These types of Christians are "ministers of misery," and they can exhaust you beyond recognition.

Ministers of Misery Examined

Are all spiritual hypochondriacs so easily spotted? Is it really true that every Christian, every minister, and every church has at least one spiritual hypochondriac in their midst? What if I really enjoy ministering to the hurting, and perhaps you, the authors of this book, are just a bit too cynical?

To resolve this question, we ask you to take this test. Years ago, Ergun heard a fellow minister give an illustration in a devotion that has remained with him to this day. See if it doesn't reveal the ministers of misery in your life.

Imagine you are returning from a long day at work. You come home weary, anticipating an evening of relaxation, when your spouse reminds you that you have a dinner date with another couple. You offer a weak objection, but she insists, so you grudgingly get dressed again and sulk out the door.

While driving to meet them, you utter those famous words every couple discusses: "How long do we have to stay before we can leave? When can we get back home, without being considered rude?"

That's right. We all say it. We just don't admit it.

So you get to the dinner date, and immediately you feel sapped of all energy. They burden you with issues, ask your opinion, and seek your help for any variety of reasons. You check your watch cautiously, and it says 8:00 PM. Three hours later, you check it again—and it is only 8:15!

Get the picture?

These people, unconsciously, are ministers of misery. They have depleted all the "resources of Christian mercy" that you have. The reason is that with these people, you have to be "on." You have to manufacture a façade. You cannot let your guard down and enjoy their company, because they are making demands on your time. The implicit understanding is that if you do not care about their most recent drama, then you are not a good Christian. You *have* to understand and you *have* to care. Thus, you manage a smile, nod your head, and pray for daylight. Add to the fact that you feel guilty for even feeling this way, and you have a dilemma.

Let's be honest. As believers in Christ, we are called to love everyone. For the most part, we do. But if we are truly honest, we have to admit that we don't always *like* everyone. Some people are predisposed to going out of their way *not* to be liked. Due to their condition, they do not *want* to be liked.

They want to be *helped*.

They are sympathy junkies, and you are their fix.

You want to tell them that the world is not as bad as they think it is. You want to remind them that in Christ we have the victory. You want to prompt them that most believers around the world have it much worse than they do, and that they should attempt to focus on the blessings of God.

But you do not. You know that you have tried before, and it was no use. Regardless of the miracle, regardless of the blessings, and regardless of the wonders of God's bounty, the "ministers of misery" seem destined to ignore your admonition and continue on in their desolation. Secretly you wonder if they are only happy when they are sad.

Compare the previous scenario to another illustration that will give a stark relief to the "ministers of misery."

You come home after a long day at work, and though you desperately want to get a nap before dinner, your spouse reminds you that you have a dinner appointment with another couple. Though you weakly offer your objections, you grudgingly get in the car. At some point during the drive, you ask the same question: "When can we leave without seeming impolite?"

This evening, however, is different. You laugh. You relax. You begin to release the tensions of the day. You genuinely feel that you can be yourself with this couple, and that they are being authentic with you. Instead of being tired and increasingly drained, you feel yourself being reenergized and filled with a second wind. At one point, you check your watch, and this time you realize that it is midnight! Where has the time gone?

These people are not ministers of misery; they are ministers of joy. Instead of depleting your reserves, they have filled you up again, and by their simple presence they have allowed you to be sharpened.

We are not suggesting that you pick and choose to whom you will minister. In every church, you must spend time ministering to the entire congregation, or at least your circle of influence. But you can choose those you want to surround yourself with. Everyone is a friend, but not everyone is a close friend. When you surround yourself with spiritual hypochondriacs, and invest most of your time with them, you will become infected. You will become drained. Those ministries of God that were at one time a joy will become a burden, and you will begin to long for a break. You will become infected with a small dose of spiritual hypochondria yourself. You cannot help it. It is infectious.

An Illustration of Remedy: Israelites in the Desert (Num. 11–14)

At the heart of the condition of a spiritual hypochondriac is that they have a lack of gratitude. Since they suffer from obsessive complaining and are infected with the "victim syndrome," they continually seek reasons for their misery. Since misery is their comfort, they are happy only when they are upset about something. Consequently, they compulsively seek reasons for their pain. It is not enough that they are unhappy; they must have a justification for their unhappiness.

To accomplish this goal, they must turn a blind eye to the obvious blessings from God in his provision. They must ignore God's favor, and focus instead on what they do not have.

There are many illustrations of a lack of gratitude in the Bible, but none is more compelling and confounding than the Israelites in the desert. Having been liberated from a four-hundred-year stint as slaves in Egypt, the Israelites were promised God's protection in the land of their fathers.

Having seen God protect them against Pharaoh's mighty army, they should have trusted that God was guiding them. God provided his continuing presence, guidance, and even daily manna to eat. Every physical need was supplied by the Lord.

This was not enough for the Israelites.

In Numbers 11, some of the Israelites responded to God's blessings with an audacity rarely exhibited in the biblical record. Moses wrote: "Contemptible people among them had a strong craving [for other food]. The Israelites cried again and said, 'Who will feed us meat? We remember the free fish we ate in Egypt, along with the cucumbers, melons, leeks, onions, and garlic. But now our appetite is gone; there's nothing to look at but this manna!'" (Num. 11:4–6).

The complaint would be laughable were it not so tragic! They were actually longing for the food they ate when they were slaves and were complaining about the manna God was providing daily for them through his sovereign love.

There were not just a few people who were complaining. This lack of gratitude, this spiritual hypochondria, was present in every home. Numbers 11:10 notes, "Moses heard the people, family after family, crying at the entrance of their tents." The poison had spread.

Moses was disturbed by the development, and he complained to the Lord. Do you question the effects of this type of hypochondria? The sheer weight of caring for ungrateful

Israelites was not only becoming a burden to Moses; he was downright suicidal. Notice Moses' prayer for death:

So Moses asked the LORD, "Why have You brought such trouble on Your servant? Why are You angry with me, and why do You burden me with all these people? Did I conceive all these people? Did I give them birth so You should tell me, 'Carry them at your breast, as a nursing woman carries a baby,' to the land that You swore to [give] their fathers? Where can I get meat to give all these people? For they are crying to me: 'Give us meat to eat!' I can't carry all these people by myself. They are too much for me. If You are going to treat me like this, *please kill me right now.* If You are pleased with me, don't let me see my misery [anymore]." (Num. 11:11–15)

Moses made a common mistake. He blamed God for the spiritual weakness of his people. God did not command the people to be ungrateful, and neither has he commanded you to contract such a disease. God offered Moses a solution, and he does the same for us.

The Lord's resolution in Moses' dilemma was to provide him with a team of seventy men who would share the burden of ministering to the whiners. These men, called "elders and officers of the people" (Num. 11:16), would be given the same anointing Moses had received which would enable them to handle the burden. Numbers 11:17 concludes with God's words: "They will help you bear the burden of the people, so that you do not have to bear it by yourself."

Amazingly, the Lord also answered their request for different foods. This is one of those rare instances when God hearkened to the whimpering complaints of an ungrateful people. But the savory meat they longed for would not meet their real need. Notice the irony of God's provision: "The LORD will give you meat and you will eat. You will eat, not for one day, or two days, or five days, or 10 days, or 20 days, but for a whole month—until it comes out of your nostrils and becomes nauseating to you—

because you have rejected the LORD who is among you, and cried to Him: 'Why did we ever leave Egypt?'" (Num. 11:18–20).

What they truly needed was to be grateful and content. Only then would they stop focusing on what they didn't have rather than God's provision.

One would imagine that God's amazing gift of food, as well as his protection of the children of God, would compel the Israelites to trust God's direction. That is not the case. A lack of gratitude always leads to a lack of faith. Indeed, why would a person trust in a God whom he believes has burdened him with a horrible life?

In Numbers 13, the twelve spies investigated the Promised Land, and returned with the report. They concluded that the land God had promised them was inhabited with armies of large men. The report of ten of the spies was that they could not conquer the land. The minority report by Joshua and Caleb was to trust God and take the land. The people chose to believe that God had brought them to the land to kill them. This is the typical response of a spiritual hypochondriac.

Their lament and lack of faith is recorded in Numbers 14:

Then the whole community broke into loud cries, and the people wept that night. All the Israelites complained about Moses and Aaron, and the whole community told them, "If only we had died in the land of Egypt, or if only we had died in this wilderness! Why is the LORD bringing us into this land to die by the sword? Our wives and little children will become plunder. Wouldn't it be better for us to go back to Egypt?" So they said to one another, "Let's appoint a leader and go back to Egypt." (Num. 14:1–4)

The result of their spiritual hypochondria was a forty-year sentence of wandering in the wilderness.

Gratitude and Healing

On the surface, the hypochondriacs in our fellowships and churches seem to be benign people. They appear to be harmless and innocent, just intent on getting a little attention. This is a deception. Do you truly understand how spiritual hypochondriacs will drag you down?

- They can drain your energy immediately.
- They can cloud any meeting, sometimes just by their presence and sour attitude.
- They can hijack your time, draining hours at a stretch.
- They drag you into their daily dramas and crises.
- They can burden you with imagined problems, keeping you from ministering to others with more pressing needs.
- They love being dependent and in need.
- They contribute little or nothing to the Lord's work, being professional complainers.

Are You Talking to Me?

Is it possible that you might be among the spiritual hypochondriacs? Could you be the chronic complainer whom others hate to see coming down the hall? If you suspect that you have succumbed to this ailment, then congratulations.

One of the clearest signs of true, malignant spiritual hypochondria is that the carrier refuses to believe he is infected. Most live in denial, assuming the entire community is conspiring against them. They feel unappreciated, unloved, and misunderstood. They consistently feel betrayed by their friends, ministers, and family. And they never realize their condition.

If you do feel that your focus has been on the negatives of your problems rather than the blessings of God, take the following five actions:

1. Focus on the blessings of God. Make it an obsession to notice the greatness and graciousness of God. In every situation, work to discover the hidden positive dimensions rather than dwelling on the problems. Notice the vast number of Scriptures where Paul concentrates on the Lord rather than himself. James 1:2 and Philippians 3 are good examples.

2. Change your thought life. Philippians 4:8 states, "Finally brothers, whatever is true, whatever is honorable, whatever is just, whatever is pure, whatever is lovely, whatever is commendable—if there is any moral excellence and if there is any praise—dwell on these things." The term *think* is an agrarian term that farmers used to describe the method by which a cow chews food. Masticating the food and constantly passing it through the four stomachs, a cow thoroughly chews food. Our thought life is the same. We are commanded to develop the discipline of carefully choosing to concentrate on those edifying things. It is a skill worthy of development.

3. Surround yourself with joyful believers. Develop relationships with those "ministers of joy" who fill you and lift you to new levels of faith and strength. Remember, their iron will sharpen your iron (Prov. 27:17).

4. Learn to pray for others. Nothing forces us to get our attention off ourselves more than learning to pray for other people's burdens. The added blessing of seeing God intervene in people's lives is mandated by God. Bearing one another's burdens fulfills the law of Christ, according to Galatians 6:2.

5. Get into a ministry now. Christian service not only gives glory to God but infuses us with a new focus—a focus on others.

Chapter 13

Diseases of the Blood and Terminal Cancers

The Blood of Christ Can Heal All
Hebrews 9:11–14

Perhaps this book has been difficult to read for some of you. In the midst of illustrations that rang true for many to whom we read the manuscript, we heard much laughter. Virtually every pastor, staff member, and member could relate to the stories we used to begin each chapter. They also had similar experiences that sparked discussions and stories.

Yes, churches can be humorous places.

But many of those leaders then lamented that these diseases were rampant in their fellowships. They would share stories of heartbreak, firings, and seemingly incurable churches where pastors and members alike were equally afflicted. They told of small lesions that became big ulcers in their churches. They spoke of the devastating effects one member, one leader, or one teacher can have on a fellowship that otherwise would be a warm and godly community of believers. Their hearts broke as they longed for that one church, that one fellowship, which could not only remain resistant to contagions, but also would know what to do when such diseases begin to spread.

What has been the common element to every discussion?

The simple question, How do any of these churches, families, and members get help? How do they find healing, when it seems like the entire world is set against them, and the diseased walk the aisles.

Surely there has to be a cure. There are healthy churches across America. There are churches which experience warmth that is inexplicable in the earthly realm. There are churches that are not like glorified lodges. There are churches that consist of believers who bear one another's burdens and thus fulfill the law of Christ (Gal. 6:2).

Perhaps you have seen that we consistently return to this seminal text in the letter that Paul wrote to the Galatians. Why is it so important? Galatians summarizes the centrality of familial support in the local church. We gather to encourage, uplift, and join shoulders. That is the biblical theory. Sadly, in practice, many churches gather to whine, complain, and fight.

Thankfully, there are churches that have recovered from devastating spiritual toxins to become what they were called to be. It is from these churches that we have learned our most meaningful lessons, and it is from these churches that we garner the content for this final chapter.

All Spiritual Diseases Are Cancers of the Blood

One continuing theme among the churches that have staved off the infection of spiritual ailments is a central belief that they are curable. They firmly believe that no disease is terminal, no matter how bleak the prognosis may be. They have a resilience that is commendable, because they do not allow the pessimistic prognoses to keep them from attempting recovery.

Second, these churches also have an aggressive method of "spiritual therapy" to deal with these issues. In virtually every case, the pastor took the lead in dealing with these illnesses. In virtually every case, he had leaders who backed him when he took a stand. One pastor had the painful task of excising a leader who was a lethal gossip. This man was connected throughout the church, and many thought that many others would follow when he left. But the pastor and the leaders decided that action was better than inaction, and when the time came, they stood united. The gossiping man did leave, but those who followed were few. The church had cauterized the wound before they lost too many others.

Finally, every church that has survived one of these lethal outbreaks viewed every spiritual malady as a form of leukemia. That is to say, they viewed every problem as a spiritual ailment rather than just a personality conflict or a confrontation between leaders. By viewing each problem as a spiritual one, they enabled the church to see it for what it really was—a leukemia or a cancer of the blood.

Christ's blood.

Christ never designed his church to be fraught with fights and problems. The apostle Paul dedicated himself not only to establishing churches but also to ensuring that they did not fall into bickering and trouble. By viewing the church as God's precious possession, no one had exclusive claims, either to the membership or the building in which the church resided. The church, they would echo, is Christ's.

If the church is Christ's and he is its foundation, then why do we always seem to fall into warfare, even within the walls of the building? Because we are not viewing ourselves as God views us. He sees us as his redeemed remnant and his voice here on earth. As long as we are alive and he postpones his coming, our purpose is clear: We are called to be his ambassadors. As ambassadors, we do not have a right to fight over our particular embassies or argue over which liaison we like best. We are to carry out the wishes of our regent who established us as a pilgrim band.

Is it too simplistic to imagine that the individual churches should remember that we are all washed in the same blood?

To say that we are redeemed by the same blood is actually not a proper perspective about the sacrifice of Christ on the cross. His regal blood, in fact, has done much more for us. The blood of Christ, according to the Bible, redeems us, sanctifies us, and enables us to live peaceably with one another. Pay close attention to the following Scripture passages. They may save your church.

The blood of Christ cleanses us from sin. "But if we walk in the light as He Himself is in the light, we have fellowship with one another, and the blood of Jesus His Son cleanses us from all sin" (1 John 1:7).

The blood of Christ obtains our eternal redemption. "He entered the holy of holies once for all, not by the blood of goats and calves, but by His own blood, having obtained eternal redemption" (Heb. 9:12).

The blood of Christ cleanses our consciences to serve him. "How much more will the blood of the Messiah, who through the eternal Spirit offered Himself without blemish to God, cleanse our consciences from dead works to serve the living God?" (Heb. 9:14).

The blood of Christ sanctifies us. "Therefore Jesus also suffered outside the gate, so that He might sanctify the people by His own blood" (Heb. 13:12).

The blood of Christ causes us to worship. "Therefore, through Him let us continually offer up to God a sacrifice of praise, that is, the fruit of our lips that confess His name" (Heb. 13:15).

The blood of Christ reconciles all to peace. "For God was pleased [to have] all His fullness dwell in Him, and through Him to reconcile everything to Himself by making peace through the blood of His cross—whether things on earth or things in heaven" (Col. 1:19–20).

Add to these the fact that Christ's blood purchased his church, according to Acts 20:28, and we see that our Lord does not take the relationships within his fellowship lightly. The writer of Hebrews goes so far as to say that the purpose of

Jesus' incarnation included his desire to show us how to withstand the tests we endure in church.

> Now since the children have flesh and blood in common, He also shared in these, so that through His death He might destroy the one holding the power of death — that is, the Devil — and free those who were held in slavery all their lives by the fear of death. For it is clear that He does not reach out to help angels, but to help Abraham's offspring. Therefore He had to be like His brothers in every way, so that He could become a merciful and faithful high priest in service to God, to make propitiation for the sins of the people. For since He Himself was tested and has suffered, He is able to help those who are tested. (Heb. 2:14–18)

In this view, heaven's temple is best perceived as the operating room for all of these lethal poisons, and nothing short of a complete "blood transfusion" is acceptable. If we truly understand Christ and his sacrifice, and view our lives as a living testimony to his sacrifice, then most of these controversies fall by the wayside. They look silly and petty in comparison.

No Simple Fixes, but Simple Answers

The solutions offered in this brief study are neither simple, nor are they easy. In an era of "least common resistance" Christianity, they demand hard action and hard decisions. One must weigh the actions and the alternatives carefully before jumping into the fray. It is important to remember that there is a right way to do things, a right time to do things, and a right spirit in which they must be enacted. To skip any of these factors can be as dangerous as the disease itself. Sometimes surgery can kill the patient if the doctor is not careful.

That having been said, the resolutions are easy to see in the light of biblical teaching. Both in the Old Testament and in the New Testament, God's leaders had little time for those who sowed seeds of discord among the brethren. If the issue was lying, then both Joshua in Joshua 7 and the apostles in Acts 5 acted quickly. So did God. When there is sin in the camp, either public or private, it can affect the entire family.

It is also important for us to note what we are *not* saying.

We are not, under any circumstance, saying that next Sunday our churches should begin to purge themselves systematically of all of the trouble-making members. After all, if each member who causes any problems were to be expunged, who would be left to turn out the lights?

Not every disease needs to be excised publicly. In fact, one of the principles that has guided churches which have survived these spiritual diseases is this: Public sin, public confession. Private sin, private confession. If all private sins were to be confessed in public, would you want to moderate that meeting?

A great example of this principle comes from our recent past. Approximately twenty years ago, a trend developed in American churches, based upon the use of "solemn assemblies." These "solemn assemblies" were well-intentioned and were based on a scriptural understanding of Joel 2:15–17:

> Blow the horn in Zion!
> Announce a sacred fast;
> proclaim an assembly.
> Gather the people;
> sanctify the congregation;
> assemble the aged;
> gather the children,
> even those nursing at the breast.
> Let the bridegroom leave his bedroom,
> and the bride her honeymoon chamber.
> Let the priests, the Lord's ministers,
> weep between the portico and the altar.
> Let them say:
> "Have pity on Your people, Lord,
> and do not make Your inheritance a disgrace,
> an object of scorn among the nations.

Why should it be said among the peoples,
'Where is their God?'"

Churches across our land took this to mean that we should gather the people in repentance and call them to confess before God our lack of humility and purity. Many of us announced to our churches that at a specific date and time, we were going to assemble ourselves and cry out before God that we did not want to hinder revival. We were willing to do whatever it took to see God bless in our midst.

In many places, that is precisely what took place. In hundreds of churches, pastors wept before their people and leaders repented before God. Churches were united as never before, as they were authentic before God and one another, many for the first time in years.

In other churches, however, the results were decidedly different. In some churches, already suffering from the onset of these spiritual diseases, the fallout had a devastating effect. We have all heard the apocryphal "pulpit legends" of confession times that got out of hand. There is a fine line between confessing our sins before God and airing our dirty laundry before the world. Some pastors spoke about men rising to microphones scattered around their auditoriums and confessing to adulterous affairs. The problem was that the women with whom they were having these affairs were seated in the church!

Should they have confessed their sins to God and been repentant? Of course. Should they have taken their sin before the entire world and shared every salacious detail? We think not. The fundamental principle was to limit the damage of such sins to as few people as possible. If we are really honest, we can imagine some members attending these solemn assemblies for the sheer pleasure of gathering more gossip to share.

In the final analysis, we must take swift and decisive action, and we must not shrink from our responsibility. The only alternative—church as usual—is no real alternative. We cannot continue as we always have. Eternity is too long, souls are too precious, and our spiritual health is too important to play games with church.

✶ It is the church for which Christ died.

He deserves a healthy body, one purged of all toxins. Besides, we operate better without these poisons, and church— real church—becomes what it was designed to be when we are cleared of these maladies. We become the family we need, the fellowship we crave, and the instrument God desires.

Chapter Study Questions

These questions are offered for discussion only. If the group leader is not careful, the discussion can quickly escalate into a fight, ironically enough. To avoid such a situation, insist that no stories include names of people, pastors, or churches. Instead, you can set the standard by including humorous stories for each example in order to avoid the more pointed issues. Steer the conversation toward the effects of actions rather than the painful actions themselves. Ask persons how they resolved the issue spiritually. Ask them to give practical advice to help others encountering similar issues. Diagnostic questions are essential because, we guarantee you, the readers will be bursting with their own examples. If you avoid discussion on a diagnostic level, it will come regardless. We are careful, however, to include biblical parameters and clues in order to guide the discussion from being a "beef" session.

Chapter 1: Toxins and Terminal Diseases in the Body of Christ

1. What do you think the average Christian family is looking for during their "church search" phase?
2. Share an experience when you were looking for a church home that you considered awkward or strange. Was the church or the church member aware that what they did was peculiar?

3. Why do you think most people are oblivious to their own symptoms of lethal Christianity?
4. The Ephesian church is called schizophrenic in the chapter. Does this make sense to you? Can a church be both visually healthy and internally sick? Excluding your present church, give an example.
5. Corinth is called a chaotic church. How would a divided church, where members are taking sides, contribute to such chaos? What is the usual result of such fights?

Chapter 2: Atrophy: Shrunken Faith and Coasting on the Past

1. Steve's mentor accused him of pastoring on autopilot, preaching the same sermons over at different congregations. How do you think this affects a church?
2. Can church members tell when a sermon is not fresh?
3. If Isaac is the portrait of unrealized potential, can you find other biblical characters that might also fit that description? Discuss your examples among the group.
4. Why does our Lord continually urge us to a daily walk of faith? Does this mitigate against coasting?

Chapter 3: Glossolitis: Swollen Tongues of Fire

1. Since gossip and slander are devastating ailments in churches, why are we so reluctant to act to stop them?
2. Share an example of gossip (excluding your present church). See if you notice a common thread among the various slanderers.
3. Do you think gossips are aware of the devastation they cause? How do gossips justify their sin? Do you think Miriam felt justified?
4. How should a church approach gossips, especially if they are active members in the church?

Chapter 4: Myopia: Nearsighted and Shortsighted

1. Consider the worst church fight you have ever seen develop in a business meeting. Discuss the aftereffects in your group.
2. In retrospect, did you notice any warning signs before the meeting that showed you that this was going to become lethal?

3. If spiritual myopia is defined as seeing only the present problem and not the future blessing, why do you think so many Christians are afflicted with the malady? Do you think the individual families invest in their own future, with investments and dreams? Why then would they see only the present cost and not the future value?

4. Do you know of other biblical examples of those who only saw the temporal problem? How did that person's shortsightedness work out?

Chapter 5: Arteriosclerosis: Harden Not Your Heart

1. Have you ever known persons who took great pride in their steadfast refusal to "come forward"?

2. Did you feel that this was due to their own spiritual power or weakness? In other words, was it because they did not need to deal with an issue, or because they did not want to deal with it?

3. Can stubbornness be both a blessing and a curse? Are there moments when being stubborn is helpful in one's Christian walk?

4. Do you believe a Christian can develop a stubborn and sinful rebellion, or do you believe such a person was never saved in the first place? Discuss your answers and deal with the issue of the sin unto death as seen in 1 John 5. For whom does God reserve that judgment?

Chapter 6: The Toxin of Bitterness: The Poison of Jealousy and Vengeance

1. Share a memory of a person who was eaten up with bitterness. Without using names, share the situation and the eventual result of this person's toxin.

2. Can refusal to release bitterness become an obsession for some people? How does it evidence itself in their lives?

3. Do you think they cling to the offense because they desire vindication, or because they want someone to "take their side"?

4. How do you feel jealousy and bitterness are related spiritual diseases? Give an example of how a person can progress through both dangerous emotions.

5. How does such a person affect the fellowship within a church?

Chapter 7: Gluttony: Always Full; Ever Empty

1. Have you ever encountered a pseudopious person, intent upon showing you his or her "holiness"? Did it ever become tragically laughable? To what extent would the person go to impress you?
2. Look again at the description of the Pharisees in Jesus' time. What symptoms would you add to the list for today?
3. We are called to holiness. This is not in question. How does the Bible distinguish between holiness and legalism?
4. Do churches today have any traditions that they view on the same level as biblical truth? Where do such things as the bulletin or the order of service fit in?

Chapter 8: Manic Depression: Ain't No Mountain High Enough

1. Have you ever known a Christian who never "leveled out"? Such persons are either on a mountaintop or in a valley. Do they ever seem content or satisfied?
2. What biblical texts would you give to a person who lacks a steady walk with God?
3. How would you approach them so as not to offend by giving your advice?
4. Jesus restored Peter, even after his manic betrayal of Jesus. Why do you think he did this?
5. Do you feel that churches are too quick to write off someone who is like Peter? Why or why not? Do you believe this is biblical restoration?

Chapter 9: The Martha Syndrome: Obsessive-Compulsive Christians

1. Consider your present church. Name the person or people who serve in the most positions, both volunteer and ascribed. Do they ever look tired to you, or do they seem to be enriched by serving in twenty capacities?
2. What do you think drives a person to work in a church, volunteering eight days a week?
3. Do you believe it is possible for a person to work too hard for the Lord? What biblical texts would you offer to prove your position?

4. Do you think it is possible that such obsessive service can have injurious effects on family life?

Chapter 10: Phobias: The Fearful and the Faithful

1. Are you the type of person who abhors public attention? Would you rather be behind the scenes than on the platform? Would you see this as a phobia or simply a personality trait?
2. Are there any other biblical characters who were paralyzed by fear? Discuss their predicaments.
3. Would you describe yourself as leaning toward a Titus-type or a Timothy-type? How do others see you?
4. Read 2 Timothy again. Do you notice Paul consistently admonishing Timothy to strength in spite of his timidity? How would you encourage someone who is spiritually phobic to trust God to conquer that fear?

Chapter 11: Anorexia and Bulimia: Eating Disorders of the Word of God

1. Do you know someone like Darlene?
2. Excluding your present pastor, describe the absolutely worst sermon you ever heard. What made that sermon so tragic? If you are a minister or teacher, share an experience in preaching or teaching that was humiliating.
3. Do you think contemporary pulpits are feeding Christians so little because the members cannot take more meat, or do you think Christians in the pew can only take so much because they have been fed a steady diet of milk?
4. How would you resolve this crisis?

Chapter 12: Hypochondria: The Gift of Discouragement

1. Read the opening section carefully. Do you know anyone who is a spiritual "cold water committee," determined to thwart any joy in church? Without using names, discuss.
2. Some choose to call such church members whiners. Why do you think some people are happy only when they complain?
3. Can a person be thankful and a perpetual complainer at the same time? Why or why not? Do you think it has an adverse effect on their own spiritual walk?

4. What are some tell-tale signs of a fault finder in the church, other than those cited in the chapter?

5. What are the adverse effects of a fault finder on a local church?

Chapter 13: Diseases of the Blood and Terminal Cancers

1. Search the New Testament for phrases that reference how members are supposed to relate to one another. Can you give five actions to which we are called, in light of "bearing one another's burdens"?

2. Galatians 6:2: "Carry one another's burdens; in this way you will fulfill the law of Christ." What do you think Paul means by this? Does it seem strange to have a "law of Christ," given the fact that Christ fulfilled the Law? Do you know of any other citations of a "law of Christ"?

3. The authors emphatically state, "Private sin, private confession. Public sin, public confession." Have you ever seen this principle violated? What were the effects of such an airing of dirty laundry?

4. Is there a difference between being accountable to one another, on the one hand, and being intrusively curious, on the other hand?